SEATTLE TRAVEL GUIDE 2023

A comprehensive updated guide to exploring the charm, sights, top attractions and hidden gems of the Emerald city

Bill Stanley

Table of contents

Chapter 1: Introduction to Seattle

Brief Seattle's history

The busy metropolis of Seattle sometimes referred to as the "Emerald City," is situated in the American Pacific Northwest. With its recognizable skyline, extensive cultural history, and spirit of entrepreneurship, Seattle has evolved from a little town to a major city with a distinctive past.

The indigenous people who have inhabited the area for countless years can be linked to Seattle's history. The region's first settlers were the Duwamish and Suquamish tribes, who made a living off the region's abounding natural resources such as salmon, cedar trees, and shellfish. The first permanent European-American settlement in what is now known as Seattle was established in 1851 by a group of settlers led by Arthur A. Denny and his party.

As a hub for the Klondike Gold Rush in the late 19th century, Seattle experienced significant expansion in its early years. The city's population increased as a result of becoming a significant supply hub for gold prospectors traveling to Alaska. Seattle swiftly developed into a vibrant commercial and cultural powerhouse as the logging and shipping industries prospered.

Seattle rose to prominence in the late 19th and early 20th century for its forward-thinking and creative attitude. The city was a hub for labor militancy, with unions battling for improved pay and working conditions. Seattle was a major hub for a radical labor organization in 1910 when the Industrial Workers of the World (IWW) held their first convention there.

Major businesses like technology and aviation also saw growth in Seattle during the early 20th century. William Boeing established the Boeing Company in 1916, and it went on to become one of the biggest aerospace producers in the world. Seattle played a crucial part in the growth of the aviation sector, notably the construction of combat aircraft during World War II, because of

Boeing's success in making the city a global aviation hub.

Seattle saw substantial economic and cultural expansion following World War II. With the emergence of businesses like Microsoft and Amazon, which have since grown to be global titans in the tech industry, the city was transformed into a hub for technology and innovation. The city of Seattle became well-known for its progressive politics, environmental activism, and thriving art scene as its economy began to diversify.

The diverse population of Seattle also reflects the city's rich cultural legacy. Longtime residents of the city include populations of immigrants from all over the world, making it a melting pot of various cultures. Today, Seattle is a distinctive and dynamic city with a rich history thanks to its thriving music industry, culinary sector, and progressive beliefs.

However, throughout its history, Seattle has also encountered difficulties. Urban development, homelessness, and racial prejudice are just a few of the problems the city has faced. A difficulty for affordable housing and social equity is the rise in inequality and housing costs brought on by rapid growth and gentrification.

Seattle continues to be a city with a rich history and a pioneering spirit despite these difficulties. It has shaped the Pacific Northwest region and had a long-lasting influence on the rest of the world as a center of invention, culture, and protest. Seattle has evolved and thrived from its earliest days as a little settlement to its present position as a global city, leaving its mark on the global stage.

Seattle's Population

Seattle's Population: A Changing Urban Environment

The lively and multicultural metropolis of Seattle also referred to as the Emerald City is situated in the Pacific Northwest region of the United States. Seattle has emerged as a leader in innovation, technology, and the arts because of its recognizable landmarks, extensive history, and progressive culture. Seattle will likely have an estimated 800,000 residents by 2023, making it the biggest city in Washington and one of the places with the highest population growth nationwide.

Historical Background

Seattle's population has an interesting past that has shaped the city's current demographics. The city was established in the middle of the 19th century, and the thriving maritime and forestry industries caused it to expand quickly in the late 1800s. Seattle developed and became a center for industry, aerospace, and technology during the beginning of the 20th century, drawing people from all over the world. Due to its robust economy, high standard of living, and diverse cultural offerings, the city has seen tremendous population expansion in recent decades.

Demographic Profile

With a population that reflects a melting pot of various nationalities, cultures, and backgrounds, Seattle is renowned for its variety. Seattle's population is roughly 65% White, 14% Asian,

8% Black or African American, 6% Hispanic or Latino, and 7% other races or multiple races, according to recent figures. Seattle is renowned for being a welcoming city for LGBTQ+ people, with a thriving LGBTQ+ community and a track record of progressive policy.

Financial and Academic Profile
One of the factors supporting Seattle's population increase is its robust economy. Numerous large firms, like Amazon, Microsoft, and Starbucks, have their headquarters in the city, offering thousands of citizens jobs. Seattle's economic vitality is also aided by the presence of top-tier educational institutions like the University of Washington and a flourishing start-up community. As a result, the city's median family income is relatively high, and a sizable portion of its citizens have advanced degrees.

Access to affordable housing
The problem of affordability, particularly in terms of housing, is one of the issues Seattle's

population must deal with. Recent increases in housing costs have made it challenging for many city dwellers to locate affordable home options. This has given rise to worries about homelessness, gentrification, and the eviction of low-income neighborhoods. However, the city has taken action to solve this issue through initiatives for affordable housing, rent control policies, and projects to enhance the supply of affordable housing.

Getting Around and Sustainability

Seattle is renowned for its dedication to environmental sustainability, and this commitment is mirrored in the city's transportation system. Buses, light rail, and ferries are all part of the city's extensive public transit network, which helps lower traffic and carbon emissions. Seattle is a walkable and bikeable city because of its wide network of bike lanes and pedestrian-friendly streets. The city has also established challenging objectives to decrease greenhouse gas emissions, boost renewable energy sources, and battle climate change.

Conclusion

People from many backgrounds make up Seattle's population, which contributes to the city's rich culture and innovative spirit. Many individuals find it to be a desirable area to live and work because of its economic prospects, commitment to sustainability, and cultural attractions. The city is attempting to solve issues including transit, housing, and affordability, but they remain major concerns. To support its expanding population and maintain its distinct identity as a preeminent American urban center, Seattle will need to remain inclusive, equitable, and sustainable as it continues to change.

Customs and traditions

Seattle, a thriving city in the Pacific Northwest of the United States, is renowned for its vibrant culture and traditions in addition to its gorgeous natural surroundings, thriving tech industry, and coffee culture. Seattle is a unique and dynamic city with a clear cultural identity because it is a melting pot of several cultures, which have inspired its arts, music, cuisine, festivals, and social standards.

One of Seattle's most important cultural characteristics is its close ties to the Native American tribes that have lived in the area for millennia. The city is situated on the ancestral territory of several tribes, including the Duwamish, Suquamish, Tulalip, and Muckleshoot. In Seattle, the rich history and customs of the area's indigenous peoples are honored and celebrated through a variety of cultural activities, galleries, and museums, including the Burke Museum and the Duwamish Longhouse and Cultural Center.

The vibrant arts community in Seattle is a crucial component of its culture. Numerous theaters, galleries, and performance venues can be found around the city where a wide variety of artistic forms, from modern art to traditional crafts, are presented. The Museum of Pop Culture, Frye Art Museum, and the Seattle Art

Museum are a few of the well-known cultural institutions that support the city's artistic heritage. Seattle's street art culture also contributes to the city's energetic and creative atmosphere with its colorful murals and graffiti.

Another essential component of Seattle's culture is music, which has had a big influence on the world music scene. Grunge, punk, and hip-hop are all deeply ingrained in the city's musical heritage, and indelible groups like Nirvana, Pearl Jam, and Soundgarden came out of the Seattle music scene in the 1990s. Innumerable venues, from tiny indie bars to enormous concert halls, feature both local and foreign musicians in Seattle today as it continues to support a robust live music scene. Another example of the city's thriving cultural landscape is the yearly Seattle International Film Festival, one of the biggest and most prestigious film festivals in the United States.

Seattle's culinary scene is renowned for its farm-to-table philosophy and focuses on locally sourced, sustainable ingredients. The city's food culture is a combination of several cuisines, from Asian delicacies to seafood from the Pacific Northwest, displaying the multicultural essence of the city. Pike Place Market is a cultural center where locals and visitors may enjoy fresh produce, artisanal food items, and regional delicacies. It is a historical landmark and one of the oldest continually operating farmers' markets in the United States.

Seattle's culture is not complete without festivals and events because they unite the neighborhood in joy. The city offers a variety of events all year long, including the Seattle International Film Festival, the well-known music and arts festival Bumbershoot, and the Northwest Folklife Festival, which highlights the various cultures and customs of the Pacific Northwest. A popular yearly event in Seattle that honors the city's nautical history is Seafair, a summer celebration that features parades, music, and boat racing.
Seattle is renowned for its ecologically sensitive society and forward-thinking social values. With

a strong emphasis on sustainability, the city has implemented programs like bike lanes, public transportation, and green spaces to lessen its carbon footprint. With a thriving LGBTQ+ community and yearly celebrations of diversity and inclusivity like the Seattle Pride Parade and PrideFest, Seattle has a reputation for being an LGBTQ+-friendly city.

Seattle's various food options, lively festivals, rich Native American heritage, thriving arts scene, prominent music culture, and forward-thinking social norms all contribute to the city's culture and traditions. The city's distinctive fusion of history, inventiveness, and progressive principles makes it a vibrant and welcoming cultural center.

Religious practices

Exploring the Different Religious Practices in the Emerald City: Religion in Seattle

Seattle is a city with a rich tapestry of religious practices in addition to being noted for its magnificent vistas, dynamic culture, and thriving tech scene. The Emerald City is a fascinating center for religious exploration and expression since it is home to a diverse population that accepts a wide variety of faiths and religious traditions.

With numerous Christian faiths spread across the city, Christianity continues to be the preeminent religion in Seattle. Other Christian religions including Protestantism, Lutheranism, and Baptist churches also have a sizable presence. The Roman Catholic Archdiocese of Seattle is in charge of many parishes. Many open and progressive Christian congregations that place a strong emphasis on social justice and environmental stewardship may be found in Seattle.

Seattle is home to an increasing number of people who follow other Abrahamic religions, such as Judaism and Islam, in addition to Christianity. Numerous synagogues and mosques

in the city serve as gathering places for Jewish and Muslim locals. To foster cooperation
and understanding between various religious groups, these faith communities actively participate in the interfaith discussion and team up on a variety of social justice activities.

Seattle is well-known for its thriving Asian religious communities in addition to its Abrahamic ones. With numerous Buddhist temples and meditation centers that provide teachings, practices, and services to both immigrants and native-born practitioners, Buddhism has a substantial presence in the city. In Seattle, some temples serve as places of prayer and venues for cultural events for the Hindu population.

Seattle has a long history of encouraging esoteric religions and spiritual inquiry. Many people are discovering spiritual disciplines like yoga, meditation, and mindfulness in the city, which is well-known for its numerous New Age and alternative spirituality communities. A large pagan culture also exists in Seattle, with practitioners of Wicca, Druidism, and other earth-based religions planning celebrations of nature and the seasons through rituals, events, and get-togethers.

In addition to its well-established religious customs, Seattle is renowned for its forward-thinking and inclusive spirituality. Organizations that encourage secular principles, critical thinking, and social activity, like the Seattle Atheists and the Humanist Society of Greater Seattle, are places where many nonreligious and secular people can find community and support.

In Seattle, several religious communities actively promote LGBTQ+ inclusion and advocacy, making it another city that accepts LGBTQ+ rights. Numerous affirming synagogues, mosques, and churches embrace LGBTQ+ people and their families and offer secure settings for worship and communal interaction.

Additionally, Seattle's devotion to social justice and sustainability frequently collides with its religious beliefs. Many faith-based organizations in the city take an active role in promoting social and environmental causes, including homelessness, racial justice, and climate change. Seattle's religious groups are renowned for their involvement in interfaith discussions, peace marches, and volunteer work, which has a positive influence on the neighborhood and beyond.

Overall, Seattle's religious landscape is varied, alive, and changing, reflecting the city's open and progressive principles. The people of Seattle actively support social justice, interreligious dialogue, and environmental sustainability and participate in a diverse spectrum of religious activities, from long-standing traditions to alternative spirituality. The diversified population of the city benefits from the city's religious communities, which makes Seattle a distinctive and vibrant center of religious practices in the Pacific Northwest.

Seattle's weather patterns

Due to climate change, Seattle, a city renowned for its stunning surroundings and pleasant weather, is seeing dramatic changes in its weather patterns. The environment of this renowned metropolis in the Pacific Northwest is changing noticeably as a result of increased temperatures, altered precipitation patterns, and sea level rise.

The rise in temperatures is one of climate change's most obvious effects in Seattle. In contrast to historical averages, the city has recently enjoyed warmer summers and milder winters. The National Oceanic and Atmospheric Administration (NOAA) reports that Seattle's yearly average temperature has risen by 0.8 degrees Celsius (or 1.5 degrees Fahrenheit) since the turn of the 20th century. Winter sports, water resources, and ecosystems that depend on snowmelt have been impacted by the city and its surroundings receiving less snow as a result of warmer temperatures.

Modifications in precipitation patterns are another key aspect of Seattle's climate change. Although the city has a reputation for being wet, changes in precipitation distribution and intensity have been brought about by climate change. According to research, Seattle is seeing more frequent and heavy rainfall events, which raises the likelihood of flooding, landslides, and stormwater overflow. Public safety, transportation, and urban infrastructure are all impacted by these catastrophes.

Seattle is becoming increasingly concerned about sea level rise. Global sea levels are rising as a result of melting glaciers, thermal expansion of seawater, and rising temperatures. Seattle is susceptible to the effects of sea level rise because it is a coastal city with numerous low-lying regions. Seattle might experience a sea level rise of up to 2.4 feet (0.73 meters) by the year 2100, which could exacerbate coastal flooding, erosion, and saltwater intrusion into freshwater supplies. Planning for cities, building infrastructure, and the health of coastal ecosystems are all affected by this.

There are social and economic repercussions of climate change in Seattle in addition to environmental ones. For instance, vulnerable populations that frequently lack access to the infrastructure and resources needed to adapt to changing conditions, such as low-income areas and communities of color, are disproportionately affected by the effects of climate change. In addition, the region's key economic sectors of agriculture, fishing, and tourism are also in danger as a result of disruptions brought on by climate change.

Seattle has been addressing climate change and preparing for its effects. To reduce greenhouse gas emissions and increase resilience to climate change impacts, the city has implemented several solutions, including green infrastructure, stormwater management systems, and climate action plans. Additionally, efforts are being undertaken to preserve and revitalize coastal habitats, including wetlands and beaches, which act as natural barriers to storm surges and sea level rise.

In conclusion, climate change is significantly affecting Seattle's climate, with the main issues being increased temperatures, altered precipitation patterns, and sea level rise. For the city and its communities, these effects have an impact on the environment, society, and the economy. To mitigate the effects of climate change and create a more sustainable future for Seattle and its residents, proactive measures like lowering greenhouse gas emissions, developing resilient infrastructure, and giving equity and social justice a top priority in climate adaptation efforts will be essential.

Top Seattle attractions

The largest city in the Pacific Northwest of the United States, Seattle, is a vibrant metropolis with a wealth of things to see and do for tourists to discover. Seattle, which is well-known for its recognizable Space Needle, coffee culture, and IT sector, has something to offer everyone. We'll examine Seattle's top attractions in further detail in this piece.

The Space Needle: Ths is one of the most recognizable sights in the world and Seattle's most identifiable landmark. This 605-foot tower, which was built in 1962, provides breathtaking views of the city and the mountains in the area. The observation deck is located at the summit, where guests can take an elevator to the top and take in the 360-degree view.

Pike Place Market: Pike Place Market is one of the nation's oldest and busiest farmers' markets. It is a fantastic location to buy artisanal goods, fresh veggies, and seafood. Visitors can also sip coffee at the original Starbucks location while watching the renowned fishmongers toss fish around.

Chihuly Garden and Glass: This gorgeous museum, which is close to the Space Needle, features the creations of renowned glass artist

Dale Chihuly. In the museum's galleries, visitors may take in Chihuly's vibrant and detailed glass sculptures; thereafter, they can explore the outside garden, which has spectacular glass pieces amidst lush greenery.

The Museum of Pop Culture, usually referred to as MoPOP, is a distinctive museum that examines the development of popular culture. Exhibitions on music, movies, television, video games, and other topics are available to visitors. Additionally, the museum has interactive displays that let guests explore and design their pop culture adventures.

The 175-foot Ferris wheel known as the Seattle Great Wheel provides stunning views of Elliott Bay and the city. Since each gondola is enclosed and climate-controlled, visitors may enjoy it all year round. While operating the wheel, visitors can also indulge in a selection of refreshments and drinks.

Otters, seals, and sharks are among the many marine animals that call the Seattle Aquarium home. Visitors can observe feeding demonstrations, interact with species from tide pools, and learn about initiatives for marine conservation.

Pioneer Square: Pioneer Square is the oldest area in Seattle and is the location of numerous historic structures and sites. Visitors have the option of taking a guided tour or going on their own, stopping at nearby eateries, boutiques, and art galleries.

The 92-acre Woodland Park Zoo is home to more than 1,000 animals from various parts of the world. In addition to learning about conservation efforts to preserve endangered species, visitors can observe lions, tigers, bears, and other exotic animals.

The Seattle Art Museum is a renowned institution that has collections of artwork from all around the world. Pablo Picasso, Georgia O'Keeffe, and Andy Warhol are just a few of the well-known painters whose works may be seen by visitors. They can also attend exhibitions that examine contemporary art and cultural history.

Hiram M. Chittenden Locks: The Hiram M. Chittenden Locks, sometimes referred to as the Ballard Locks, are a network of canals and locks that enable boats to navigate between the freshwater of Lake Union and Lake Washington and the saltwater of Puget Sound. Visitors can explore the nearby botanical gardens while watching boats navigate the locks.

Seattle is a city that invites tourists to experience a variety of attractions. There is something for everyone in this dynamic city, from recognizable landmarks like the Space Needle to distinctive attractions like the Museum of Pop Culture.

Islands in Seattle

Seattle's Islands: A Paradise in the Pacific Northwest

A network of islands around Seattle, Washington, which is noted for its breathtaking natural beauty and provides both locals and tourists with a singular and scenic experience. Seattle's islands are a refuge for nature lovers and outdoor enthusiasts, offering everything from rocky vistas to serene beaches. Let's examine some of the islands that make up this paradise in the Pacific Northwest in more detail.

Bainbridge Island is a well-liked location for day trips or weekend getaways. It is only a short ferry ride from downtown Seattle. This lovely island features modest boutiques, art galleries, and cafes that give off a small-town vibe. Visitors can ride bikes to cruise the island's gorgeous landscapes, visit the island's clean beaches, and climb through lush woodlands. Bainbridge Island is a great location for wine lovers because it has many wineries as well.

The largest island in the San Juan Islands archipelago, Orcas Island is home to rough coasts, thick forests, and breathtaking mountain panoramas. Orcas Island, which is well-known for its pristine environment and outdoor recreation possibilities, provides a variety of activities like hiking, kayaking, and whale watching. There are several galleries and studios to visit on the island, which also boasts a thriving art scene. With its stunning lakes, waterfalls, and expansive vistas from the top of Mount Constitution, Moran State Park on Orcas Island is a must-see location.

Vashon Island is a relaxed, rural haven close to Seattle that is renowned for its eccentric appeal and creative culture. The island is a hub for farm-to-table dining and distinctive shopping because it is home to various farms, wineries, and local artists. Visitors can enjoy leisurely bike rides along the island's gorgeous roads, stroll through its woodlands, or explore the island's stunning beaches. Vashon Island is renowned for having a thriving arts scene with a wide variety of galleries, theaters, and music venues.

Whidbey Island is the largest island in Washington State and is situated north of Seattle.

It features a variety of scenery, including lush forests and sandy beaches. The island is well-known for its quaint seaside towns, interesting landmarks, and stunning scenery. In addition to visiting the famous Deception Pass Bridge and the lovely trails of the Ebey's Landing National Historical Reserve, tourists can stroll through the charming villages of Langley and Coupeville. Numerous state parks on Whidbey Island are also located there and provide camping, boating, and wildlife viewing possibilities.

Blake Island is a distinctive site in Puget Sound recognized for its rich cultural history and scenic beauty. Tillicum Village, a Native American cultural hub where visitors can learn about the extensive history and customs of the Coast Salish people, is located on the island. The island also provides camping, beachcombing, and beautiful hiking routes.

Tourists can discover a wide variety of landscapes, activities, and cultural experiences on Seattle's islands. These islands are a haven for outdoor enthusiasts, art aficionados, and those looking for a tranquil escape from the hectic city life thanks to their immaculate beaches and deep forests. Seattle's islands are an undiscovered Pacific Northwest paradise with their stunning landscapes, little towns, and distinctive attractions.

Chapter 2: Planning your trip

Cost evaluation

Tourists looking for a distinctive experience in the Pacific Northwest frequently travel to Seattle, which is well-known for its breathtaking natural beauty, vibrant culture, and growing tech scene. To ensure a cost-effective trip to Seattle without sacrificing pleasure, it is crucial to take financial considerations into account while making travel plans. Here is detailed advice on how a tourist might budget for a trip to Seattle.

Accommodations: There are many different places to stay in Seattle, including hotels, motels, rental homes, and hostels. The price of lodging varies according to the area, extras, and time of year. In contrast to districts like Capitol Hill, Fremont, and Ballard, downtown Seattle often has higher prices. Find the best lodging for your budget by doing some research and comparing several possibilities.

Public transportation: Seattle has a robust system that includes buses, light rail, and ferries. Your itinerary and the locations you intend to visit will determine how much your transportation will cost. Consider getting a Seattle CityPASS, which covers unlimited public transportation and cheap entrance to popular attractions. If you want to travel outside of Seattle, another option is to rent a car, though parking costs can mount up quickly. When creating your budget, take transportation costs into account.

Food: From fresh seafood to craft coffee, Seattle is renowned for its eclectic cuisine scene. Spending money on eating out might be big, so plan properly. To save money, think about eating at nearby cafes, food trucks, and inexpensive restaurants. Experiencing Seattle's gastronomic choices on a budget can also be accomplished by going to regional farmers' markets. Additionally, cooking your meals while staying in a vacation rental can be a budget-friendly choice.

Attractions include the Space Needle, Pike Place Market, museums, and parks. Seattle also has a wide variety of other attractions. Prioritize the attractions you want to see and do some research on the admission costs. To avoid paying admission fees, look for tickets that are on sale or combo packages. Planning your visits properly will help you make the most of your money since many attractions also provide free or discounted admission on particular days or at particular times.

Outdoor activities: One of Seattle's top draws is the surrounding natural splendor, which offers opportunities for hiking, biking, and national park exploration. While many outdoor pursuits are free, some could call for leases or licenses. Make plans based on your research into the costs involved with outdoor activities. Given that Seattle's weather may be erratic, investing in outdoor equipment like rain jackets and durable shoes can also be a smart move.

Shopping and souvenirs: Seattle has a thriving retail sector with distinctive boutiques, artisan markets, and souvenir stores. Set a spending limit for mementos and retail therapy and stick to it. For inexpensive and unusual treasures, check out your neighborhood markets and thrift shops.

Budgeting for extra costs like gratuities, taxes, Wi-Fi, and unplanned charges is important. You can stay on track if your budget includes a reserve for unforeseen costs.

Seasonal factors: The climate in Seattle varies significantly from season to season. The shoulder seasons of spring (March to May) and fall (September to November) may provide better rates, although the summer months (June to August) often are the main tourist season with higher prices. Although the winter months of December through February might be cold and rainy, they also have reasonable prices. When organizing your trip to Seattle, take the season into account to minimize your expenses.

Exchange rates and credit card fees should be taken into consideration if you are traveling to Seattle from another nation. Check with your credit card company about overseas transaction fees and do your research on the best currency conversion possibilities. You can avoid paying extra fees by using credit cards with no international transaction fees.

Budget for two

Seattle, a thriving metropolis in the Pacific Northwest of the United States, is renowned for its breathtaking natural beauty, rich cultural diversity, and thriving arts scene. To help you budget and make the most of your trip, it's necessary to get a general idea of the average cost if you're planning a trip to Seattle with your two-person family. Here is a thorough summary of the expected average cost for a family of two visiting Seattle, including lodging, travel, food, and activities.

Accommodation:
Depending on the kind of property you select and where it is located, the cost of lodging in Seattle might vary significantly. A mid-range hotel room in Seattle will typically run you

between $150 and $250 a night. However, at busy times or during special occasions, costs could increase. As an alternative, you can select less expensive lodgings like motels or hostels, which can range in price from $70 to $150 per night. High-end lodging options, such as hotels or vacation homes, might run you upwards of $300 per night if you choose a more opulent stay.

Transportation:
Buses, light rail, and streetcars are all part of Seattle's well-connected public transit network, which makes moving around the city both simple and economical. An individual day pass for public transit costs about $8. Depending on the kind of vehicle and insurance coverage, you might anticipate paying anywhere between $50 and $100 per day if you choose to rent a car. It's crucial to pay for parking costs as well because they may be fairly high in downtown Seattle.

Meals: The vibrant food scene in Seattle is well-known for its vast selection of delectable dishes, including seafood, farm-to-table fare, and international flavors. Without including alcoholic beverages, a meal for two in a mid-range restaurant in Seattle can run you anywhere from $40 to $80. You can get a fast bite at food trucks or informal restaurants for about $10 to $15 per person if you prefer a more affordable choice. Depending on your eating habits and nutritional choices, the cost of groceries for preparing your meals might range from $100 to $150 each week.

Attractions:

A wide range of attractions is available in Seattle to suit all interests and price ranges. The entrance costs for well-known attractions including the Space Needle, Pike Place Market, and the Museum of Pop Culture (MoPOP) range from $20 to $40 per person. Costs range from $10 to $30 per person for trips to Bainbridge Island or the Seattle Aquarium. When it comes to transportation and park fees, a trip to Mount Rainier National Park or a boat ride to the San Juan Islands can run you $30 to $50 per person.

Supplemental Charges:

Budgeting for supplemental costs like souvenirs, snacks, and other products is crucial. Small trinkets can cost $5 while specialty items can cost $100 or more. Depending on how much you consume, snacks and drinks can run you anywhere from $5 to $10 per person every day. Setting aside money for unforeseen costs or emergencies is also a good idea.

Depending on your choice of lodging, transportation, meals, and activities, the expected average cost for a family of two visiting Seattle can range from $1500 to $3000 for a 3–4 day trip. It's crucial to remember that costs might change based on the time of year, supply, and individual preferences. Always do your study, make your plans in advance, and create a budget that works for your means. Seattle is a city worth visiting because of its distinctive attractions and lively culture, and by planning your finances well, you may maximize your family trip.

Budget for three

For families looking for an exciting holiday, Seattle, which is well-known for its breathtaking natural beauty, vibrant cultural scene, and cutting-edge tech industry, is a popular choice. To properly plan your budget if you're taking a family of three to the Emerald City, it's critical to grasp the typical expenditures involved with such a trip.

Accommodation:
Depending on the location, season, and type of lodging you select, the cost of lodging in Seattle can vary significantly. A mid-range hotel room in Seattle can often run you between $150 and $250 per night. However, you can come across more affordable choices or deluxe lodgings that drastically raise the price. Alternatives include holiday rentals like Airbnb, where prices for a small apartment or house typically range from $100 to $200 per night.

Transportation:

Your travel to Seattle may incur additional transportation expenses. If you're coming by plane, you'll need to factor in the price of flights for three people, which might change depending on the airline, the departure city, and the time of booking. Domestic travel inside the US can range in price from $200 to $500 per person, one-way. When you arrive in Seattle, you might also need to set aside money for local transportation. Buses, light rail, and ferries are all part of Seattle's large public transit network, which includes fares as low as $3 per trip or $6 for a day pass. Another choice is to rent a car, although this will incur extra expenses for gas, tolls, and parking.

Food:
Eating out may be expensive for a family of three, despite Seattle's reputation for its diverse culinary scene. Excluding drinks, tax, and tips, a meal at a mid-range restaurant in Seattle can go between $15 to $30 per person on average. Dining out for breakfast, lunch, and dinner for a few days can add up rapidly for a family of

three. If you have access to a kitchen in your lodging, you may want to try making your meals or eating at more affordable restaurants.

Attractions:

Families may enjoy a variety of activities in Seattle, including well-known locations like the Space Needle, Pike Place Market, and the Seattle Aquarium. These sites have a range of admission prices, with the Space Needle charging about $30 for adults and $20 for children and the Seattle Aquarium charging about $30 for adults and $20 for children. There may be additional costs for excursions, museums, parks, and other attractions. To prevent unforeseen costs during your vacation, it's advisable to budget for these charges in advance.

All Other Expenses:

It's also important to include supplemental costs for your trip, such as food, souvenirs, and incidentals. In Seattle, which is known for its coffee culture, a cup of coffee can run you anywhere from $3 to $5. Budgeting a little extra cash for souvenirs and other expenses is a good idea because these costs may quickly add up.

Conclusively,several variables might affect the average cost of a trip to Seattle for a family of three, including lodging, travel, food, attractions, and other costs. In general, you may anticipate lodging prices of $150 to $250 per night, airfares of $200 to $500 per person, meals at mid-range restaurants of $15 to $30 per person, and additional fees for attractions, transportation, and other incidental expenses. To guarantee you have a fun trip without going over budget, it's essential to plan, study costs, and make a budget. Making the most of your family's trip to Seattle and making priceless memories in the Emerald City is possible with careful planning and budgeting.

Best times to visit Seattle

Seattle, a bustling American city located in the Pacific Northwest, is home to many tourist attractions, including the famous Space Needle and the scenic waterfront. Timing is essential when booking a trip to Seattle because the city has different seasons and weather all year long. So when is the ideal time to travel to Seattle? Explore now.

Summertime (June through August)
In Seattle, the summer is the busiest travel period, and for good reason. With temperatures between the mid-60s and low 70s Fahrenheit (15-24°C), the weather during this time of year is at its best. There is plenty of time to explore the city and its surroundings because of the long days and longer daylight hours. The famed Seafair with its hydroplane racing and air shows and the renowned Seattle International Film Festival are just two of the many outdoor activities and festivals that take place in Seattle during the summer. Additionally, it's a great time to go hiking, ride, and explore the parks and shoreline of the city. Summertime is the ideal time to visit well-known tourist destinations like Pike Place Market and take a ferry ride to adjacent islands.
September to November:

With the foliage turning color and the air beginning to chill off, fall is a gorgeous season in Seattle. With temperatures in the 60s Fahrenheit (15-20°C) in September, the city's outdoor attractions are ideal for enjoyment without the heaviest summer crowds. The city's autumn foliage is at its finest in October and November, when temperatures drop to the mid-50s Fahrenheit (10–15°C) and provide breathtaking vistas for nature lovers. The city's cultural scene also comes alive in the fall, with events like the Earshot Jazz Festival and the Seattle International Comedy Competition.

December through February is winter.
Seattle's winters are known for their frigid temperatures, continuous rain, and sporadic snowfall. During this time of year, the average temperature falls between the mid-40s and low-50s Fahrenheit (4-10°C). Winter in Seattle can, despite the chilly conditions, be a lovely time to visit. During the Christmas season, the city is decked out in cheery lights and ornaments, and must-see events include the

Pacific Northwest Ballet's "The Nutcracker" and the Seattle Center Winterfest. Additionally, fewer people are present throughout the winter, which results in shorter waits at well-known tourist attractions like the Space Needle and Pike Place Market. Indulge in the city's culinary scene during this season, when quaint eateries serve hearty meals.

March to May:
Seattle is especially lovely in the spring when the weather begins to warm up and cherry blossoms and other flowers begin to bloom, bringing life to the city's vegetation. May provides drier weather with temperatures in the mid-50s to mid-60s Fahrenheit (10-18°C), which contrasts with the often rainy and occasionally showery conditions of March and April. Seattle's springtime blooms, including those at the renowned Washington Park Arboretum and the University of Washington's cherry blossoms, are great for anyone who enjoy the outdoors and the natural world. The city's bustling areas, such as Fremont and Capitol Hill, with their distinctive

stores, cafes, and galleries, are also fantastic times to explore.

Finally, when to travel to Seattle depends mainly on individual choices and interests. The warmest months are summer and fall, when there are many outdoor activities and events to choose from as well as spectacular autumnal foliage. While spring gives lovely flowers and pleasant weather, winter offers a special holiday appeal and fewer visitors. Seattle is a great place to visit all year round because it has something to offer visitors looking for a unique experience, regardless of the season they select.

To enter Seattle, does one needs a visa?

It's important to be informed of the visa requirements if you're considering a vacation to Seattle, a stunning city in the Pacific Northwest of the United States. While many visitors from around the world can visit Seattle without a visa, some individuals must obtain one to do so.

Non-U.S. Citizens: Seattle typically requires a visa for visitors from outside the United States. This comprises visitors from several nations, including China, India, Brazil, and Mexico. The kind of visa you need will depend on whether you're traveling for business, pleasure, employment, or academic purposes. It's crucial to examine the U.S. For information on the precise visa requirements and application procedure, consult the Department of State website or get in touch with the American embassy or consulate in your nation.

Nationals of nations participating in the Visa Waiver Program (VWP) are permitted to travel to the United States for up to 90 days without a visa under the VWP, which is a policy that has been put in place by the country. However, visitors from VWP nations who intend to stay in Seattle for more than 90 days or a different reason, like a job or study, will require a visa. It's crucial to keep in mind that, even if you are from a VWP nation, you must still apply for permission through the Electronic System for

Travel Authorization (ESTA) before your journey to the United States.

Refugees and Asylees: Refugees and Asylees are qualified to travel to Seattle without a visa if they have been granted asylum in the United States. To enter the United States, you must have the required documentation, such as your refugee travel document or asylee travel document.

Children and Spouses of U.S. Citizens: Spouses and kids of U.S. citizens may be eligible for a visa, such as an immigrant visa or a K visa if they are going to Seattle to join a U.S. citizen family member. These visas enable family members to go to the country permanently, live and work there, or be married to a citizen of the country before requesting permanent residency. However, because applying for these visas can be difficult and time-consuming, it's advised to seek legal counsel or advice from the American embassy or consulate.

People with Special Circumstances: Some people may need a visa to visit Seattle because of their unique circumstances, such as medical emergencies, humanitarian needs, or diplomatic missions. The U.S. embassy or consulate should be contacted for advice and assistance as these situations are handled on an individual basis.

Summarily, even though a lot of tourists can visit Seattle without a visa, some individuals must apply for one before their trip. Non-U.S. Seattle may require a visa for citizens, citizens of VWP countries going for a different purpose or staying longer than 90 days, refugees and asylees, spouses and children of U.S. citizens, and anyone with unique circumstances. It's essential to confirm the particular visa requirements and application process depending on your unique situation, and if necessary, obtain legal advice. A hassle-free journey to Seattle will be made possible by advanced planning and knowledge of the visa requirements.

How to obtain a visa to visit Seattle

Application for a Visa in Seattle: A Complete Guide for Travelers

Depending on your place of origin, you might need to apply for a visa if you're a foreign visitor intending to visit Seattle, Washington. A visa is a legal document that enables you to travel to and remain in the United States for a predetermined reason, such as business, tourism, or study. In this thorough guide, we'll walk you through the procedures for obtaining a Seattle visa so you may travel easily and without a problem.

Identify the Visa Type You Need: The first step in obtaining a Seattle visa is to identify the visa type you require. The B1/B2 tourist visa and the F1 student visa are the two most popular types of visas for visitors visiting Seattle. The F1 visa is for students engaged in academic programs, whereas the B1/B2 visa is for brief visits for tourism, business, or medical treatment.

Get the Required Documents: After determining the type of visa you require, you must acquire the necessary paperwork. Depending on the type of visa, precise documentation may vary, but in general, you'll need a current passport, a completed visa application form, a passport-sized photo, documentation of your travel arrangements, and financial proof demonstrating your ability to sustain yourself while you're in the United States. Additional paperwork, such as a letter of invitation, documentation of your ties to your country of origin, and proof that you intend to return home after your visit, may be required.

Fill out the online visa application form: Once you've gathered all the necessary paperwork, you'll need to do so. The U.S. is used for this. You must enter personal data, travel information, and other pertinent facts on the Department of State's website. Before submitting the form, make sure your entries are accurate and comprehensive.

Once you have finished filling out the online application, you must pay the visa application fee. Regardless of whether your visa application is approved or denied, the cost amount varies based on the type of visa and is not refundable. You must preserve the receipt as proof of payment and can pay the cost online with a credit card or another acceptable method.

Schedule and Attend a Visa Interview You must schedule a visa interview at the U.S. Consulate after paying the visa application fee. Consulate or embassy in your country of origin. An important part of the application procedure is the visa interview, which enables a consular official to assess your eligibility for a visa. Be ready to discuss your intended itinerary, the reason for being there, and your financial position. Bring all pertinent documents with you to the interview as you might be asked to give more during that time.

Await Visa Approval or Denial: The consular officer will decide whether to grant or deny your visa after your interview. If accepted, you will get a visa stamped in your passport allowing you to visit the United States. If your application is rejected, the consular official will explain their decision to you. You might be eligible to submit a new application for a visa or file an appeal in specific circumstances.

Prepare for Travel: You can start getting ready for your trip to Seattle if your visa application is granted. Make sure to reserve your transportation, lodging, and other travel-related needs, and be prepared to display your passport and visa stamp at the U.S. port of entry. To ensure a smooth entry into the country, don't forget to educate yourself about U.S. immigration laws and customs processes.

Is a trip to Seattle worthwhile?

Seattle, Washington, is the only city you need to consider if you're seeking a distinctive and exciting vacation spot. Seattle, a city in the stunning Pacific Northwest of the United States, is home to a wide range of attractions for tourists to take advantage of. A trip to Seattle is unquestionably worthwhile because of the city's famous landmarks, vibrant artistic community, and an array of dining options. These strong arguments should convince you to visit Seattle.

Seattle is surrounded by breathtakingly beautiful natural scenery. The city has breathtaking beauty that will astound you, with the imposing Mount Rainier serving as its backdrop and the glistening waters of Puget Sound. To enjoy the area's breathtaking natural beauty up close, you can take a ferry ride to adjacent islands, stroll along the picturesque waterfront, or visit the many beautiful parks and gardens. Seattle's natural splendor will enthrall you whether you enjoy the outdoors or merely beautiful scenery.

Seattle is home to many famous landmarks that are a must-see for tourists. One of Seattle's most recognizable landmarks, the Space Needle, provides panoramic views of the city and its surroundings from its observation deck. The Chihuly Garden and Glass is a distinctive and all-encompassing art experience that displays the magnificent glass creations of renowned artist Dale Chihuly. You can eat local fare, watch fishmongers throw fish, and buy one-of-a-kind products at the Pike Place Market, a historic farmer's market with a view of Elliott Bay. These sites are just a few illustrations of the city's rich culture and history, which contribute to its value as a travel destination.

Arts & Culture: Any traveler with a passion for creativity will be delighted by Seattle's vibrant arts and cultural scene. As the site of renowned music events like Bumbershoot and the origin of grunge music, the city is renowned for its thriving music scene. You can see live concerts at a variety of music venues or visit the Museum of Pop Culture (MoPOP), whose interactive exhibits celebrate popular culture. The Seattle Art Museum (SAM) is home to an extraordinary collection of both traditional and modern artwork from all over the world. The city is also filled with theaters, galleries, and public artworks that showcase its extensive artistic legacy.

Culinary Delights: With a diversified culinary scene that appeals to all tastes, Seattle is a food lover's heaven. Everyone may find something to enjoy in the city, from farm-to-table meals to fresh seafood. You may savor regional favorites like clam chowder, Dungeness crab, and handcrafted chocolates at Pike Place Market, a culinary treasure trove. The International District has a wide selection of Asian restaurants, while Capitol Hill is well-known for its hip eateries and specialty martini lounges. Seattle is a sanctuary for coffee lovers as well, with many coffee shops selling the city's renowned specialty coffee. It will be a joy for your taste buds to explore Seattle's culinary scene.

Outdoor experiences: The Pacific Northwest, where Seattle is located, is a great place for outdoor experiences. You can go hiking in the neighboring mountains, bike along the Burke-Gilman Trail for a beautiful view, or kayak in Puget Sound. The city also offers a lot of parks and green areas, like Gas Works Park and Discovery Park, where you can go for a leisurely run or picnic. Seattle's natural playground is likely to enthrall outdoor enthusiasts.

The Atmosphere of Friendship and Hospitality: Seattle is renowned for its atmosphere of friendship and hospitality. "Seattleites," as the locals are referred to, are renowned for their friendly demeanor and carefree outlook. You'll discover a multicultural and accepting neighborhood that values many beliefs, ways of life, and civilizations. If you're wondering about the city's neighborhoods or

Required shots to get before traveling

Why Mandatory Vaccinations are Important for Visitors to Seattle

Vaccinations have become an essential weapon in the struggle to stop the spread of the COVID-19 pandemic as the globe struggles to cope with its problems. Seattle, famed for its vibrant culture, gorgeous beauty, and bustling tourism scene, is no different from other towns and tourist attractions throughout the world in that it has put in place measures to protect its citizens and visitors. As a result, mandatory vaccinations are now a requirement for visitors coming to Seattle to protect everyone's health and safety.

Seattle, a city in the Pacific Northwest of the United States, is a well-liked vacation spot because of its well-known attractions including the Space Needle, Pike Place Market, and stunning shoreline. Every year, the city welcomes millions of visitors from around the globe, making it essential to implement strict health and safety regulations. Mandatory vaccinations for visitors to Seattle are intended to protect not only the visitors' health but also the local population, lower the danger of disease transmission, and preserve the city's general public health.

The Seattle city government made vaccines for visitors a requirement in part to control the spread of contagious diseases. It has been demonstrated that vaccines are efficient at preventing the spread of communicable diseases, especially respiratory conditions like COVID-19. Seattle wants to reduce the danger of outbreaks and safeguard vulnerable groups from possible exposure to contagious diseases, such as the elderly and those with underlying medical issues, by requiring vaccinations for visitors.

Additionally, Seattle requires visitors to receive certain immunizations to protect the local population. There is a larger chance of infection transmission when tourists mingle with locals in places like hotels, restaurants, and public transportation. The load on the local healthcare system is lessened and the health and well-being of the city's citizens have been protected thanks to vaccination laws that make visitors less likely to carry and spread diseases.

The maintenance of the city's general public health is a significant component of Seattle's requirement that visitors receive certain vaccines. Disease outbreaks can have a big economic and societal impact, from higher healthcare expenses to lost income and productivity. Seattle wants to prevent possible disease outbreaks that can harm the community's economy and place a burden on public health resources by implementing vaccination regulations. To keep Seattle's citizens and visitors healthy and to keep the city a desirable and secure tourism destination, vaccinations are an essential preventive precaution.

Additionally, overseas visitors must get the required vaccines before visiting Seattle. Depending on their public health laws, several nations have varied immunization mandates. By requiring vaccinations before travel, Seattle can assure adherence to global health standards and stop the importation and international spread of disease. This helps guard against any health concerns brought on by travel for both tourists and the local population.

It is important to remember that additional routine vaccines advised by public health authorities may potentially be required for travelers visiting Seattle in addition to the COVID-19 vaccine. These could include immunizations against diseases like hepatitis, measles, mumps, and rubella. These immunizations are essential for preserving public health and lowering the danger of epidemics, particularly in areas where travelers from other countries congregate.

Conclusively, mandatory vaccinations for visitors to Seattle are an essential step in ensuring everyone's health and safety in the city. They support preventing the transmission of infectious diseases, protect the neighborhood, uphold the city's general public health, and guarantee adherence to global health standards. A tried-and-true method for stopping the spread of disease and lowering the likelihood of outbreaks is vaccination. Tourist vaccination regulations will probably continue to be an important part of travel and tourism policies while the globe struggles to deal with the effects of the COVID-19 pandemic.

Winter gears

With its snow-covered vistas and brisk, bracing air, winter in Seattle can be lovely and entrancing. With severe rain, icy temperatures, and sporadic snowstorms, it can also be unpredictable and difficult. It's crucial to be ready with the appropriate equipment and apparel if you're planning a winter trip to Seattle to keep warm, dry, and secure. Here is a detailed list of winter gear that every visitor to Seattle needs to pack.

Seattle is known for its rain, and the winter months may be particularly wet. To protect yourself from the rain, make sure to bring a high-quality waterproof jacket with a hood. For the best defense, look for a jacket with sealed seams and a durable water-repellent (DWR) coating. To keep your lower body dry in case of heavy snowfall or rain, it is also advised to wear waterproof boots and jeans.

Warm Insulating Layers: In cold weather, layering is essential for keeping warm. Layers of warmth, like fleece coats, thermal tops, and sweaters, should be brought along in abundance. Choose textiles like wool or synthetics that will keep you warm even when they become wet. Additionally, it's a good idea to pack extra layers that you may add or take off as the weather warrants.

Waterproof footwear is necessary to keep your feet warm and dry during Seattle's occasionally wet and snowy winters. To avoid slipping and falling on slick surfaces, invest in waterproof footwear with strong traction. For more warmth and comfort, go for insulated boots.

Hat, Gloves, and Scarf: To shield your extremities from the brisk wind and chilly temperatures, remember to take a warm hat, pair of gloves, and scarf. To keep your head, hands, and neck warm and protected, look for clothing composed of insulating fabrics such as fleece or wool.

Thermal Socks: In Seattle's winter, keeping your feet warm and dry is essential. For dry, warm feet even in wet conditions, bring thermal socks made of moisture-wicking fabrics like merino wool or synthetic fibers.

Sunglasses: Even though they may seem illogical, sunglasses are a necessity for Seattle's winter weather. Winter sun at a low angle can be blinding, especially when it reflects off of wet or snowy surfaces. Bring UV-protective sunglasses with you so that you can screen your eyes from glare and dangerous UV rays.

Emergency Kit: The winter season might occasionally bring unforeseen difficulties, therefore it's crucial to be ready with an emergency kit. Include in your emergency bag things like a flashlight, additional batteries, a first aid kit, hand warmers, a multi-tool, and a whistle. Having a fully charged power bank for your phone in case of emergency is also a good idea.

Bring rain gear if you intend to use your camera or other electronic equipment while you are traveling to protect it from moisture. In wet weather, waterproof cases for various electronic gadgets, phone pouches, and camera rain covers can assist keep them dry and functional.

Navigational Aids: Seattle's winter weather occasionally causes decreased visibility, particularly during snowstorms or periods of intense rain. If you intend to go trekking or explore the outdoors, bring navigational aids like a compass and a waterproof map to help you find your way around.

Extra Food and drink: Having extra food and drink on hand is always a good idea in case of unforeseen delays or emergencies. Bring a reusable water bottle and high-energy snacks like almonds, granola bars, and dried fruits with you on your winter travels to remain hydrated.

Summer gears

Seattle's summer is a time of exhilarating outdoor recreation and magnificent scenery. The Emerald City provides a wealth of chances for visitors to explore and delight in the great outdoors thanks to its temperate climate and breathtaking vistas. Here are the five summer essentials that every visitor to Seattle needs to make the most of their vacation.

Wear rain gear because Seattle is renowned for its overcast skies, even in the summer. Don't let the rain bring you down! Bring an umbrella, a sturdy raincoat, and water-resistant footwear. While enjoying the city's parks, gardens, and shoreline, will guarantee that you remain dry and comfortable.

Sunscreen: The sun can still be intense, especially during the hottest times of the day, even if Seattle may not be known for its sweltering summers. To protect your skin from damaging UV rays, be sure to pack high-quality sunscreen with at least SPF 30 or higher. Apply it liberally to your face, arms, neck, and any other exposed skin.

Comfortable Walking Shoes: With its hilly streets and lovely neighborhoods, Seattle is a city suited for walking. A pair of relaxed walking shoes that will keep your feet pleased while you explore should be in your luggage. To ensure a comfortable and pain-free experience while exploring the city, choose shoes with strong arch support and cushioning.

Water bottle: It's important to stay hydrated, especially in the summer heat. A reusable water bottle is a necessity if you want to stay hydrated and rejuvenated while exploring Seattle. The numerous public water faucets and drinking stations dotted across the city make it simple to refill it.

Blanket for a picnic: Seattle has a lot of lovely parks and green areas that are ideal for a leisurely lunch. Bring a light picnic blanket or mat and some refreshments, and have a leisurely picnic in Seattle's scenic surroundings. The best places to spread out a blanket and take in the surroundings are well-known locations like Gas Works Park, Green Lake Park, and Kerry Park.

Use your camera or smartphone to capture the beauty of Seattle's magnificent cityscapes, well-known landmarks, and amazing views. Bring your camera or smartphone with you so you may document the beauty of the city. There are many picture-perfect moments, from the well-known Space Needle to the breathtaking Mount Rainier in the distance, to capture and share with friends and family.

Sunglasses and a hat: It's necessary to protect your eyes and face from the sun, so these two summertime accessories are a must. Select sunglasses with UV protection and a hat with wide brim to shield your face and neck from the sun. They won't just keep you comfy; they'll also lessen your danger of becoming sunburned and having UV rays harm your eyes.

Although mosquitoes may not be a major issue in Seattle, there may still be some bothersome bugs, especially in wooded regions or close to bodies of water. If you bring a bug spray with DEET or other efficient insect repellents, you can help keep those pesky insects away and continue to enjoy your outdoor activities uninterrupted.

Dress in layers because Seattle's weather may change quickly, especially in the summer. Layered clothing, such as lightweight jackets or sweaters, is usually a good option because temperatures might drop at night or when you're near the sea. By layering, you can simply change your outfit in response to the weather and remain cozy all day.

Modes of getting to Seattle

Seattle, Washington, a bustling city famous for its breathtaking waterfront, iconic Space Needle, and thriving cultural scene, is located in the picturesque Pacific Northwest region of the

United States. This thorough post will give you a variety of options to make your trip to Seattle easy and pleasurable if you're wondering how to get there and are planning a trip there.

By Air:

The principal airport serving the city is Seattle-Tacoma International Airport (SEA), also referred to as Sea-Tac. Seattle is easily reached by plane thanks to its excellent connections to significant cities both domestically and abroad. Direct flights from a variety of domestic and international locations are provided by several significant carriers to Seattle. You can hire a car, take a shuttle, or use buses or the Link light rail to travel to downtown Seattle or other parts of the city after landing at Sea-Tac.

In a train:

Taking the train is a wonderful choice if you want scenic travel. Amtrak provides long-distance train services to Seattle from numerous American locations, including the well-known Coast Starlight route, which travels from Los Angeles to Seattle and provides breathtaking views of the Pacific coastline. The Empire Builder route of Amtrak also links Seattle and Chicago while traveling through several breathtaking national parks. You may easily use the city's public transportation choices or rent a car to explore the area further after arriving at the iconic King Street Station in downtown Seattle.

By Car:

A road trip is an interesting choice because Seattle is well connected to the rest of the United States by a system of highways. Take Interstate 5 (I-5) through Seattle if you're traveling by car from adjacent locations like Portland or Vancouver, Canada. Another well-traveled route that provides spectacular coastal vistas on the way to Seattle is Highway 101, often known as the Pacific Coast Highway. Be aware that parking in downtown Seattle can be scarce and expensive, especially during rush hours, and that traffic congestion may occur.

By Bus:

Many bus companies run economical and practical transit to Seattle. The largest intercity bus company in North America, Greyhound, provides trips to Seattle from numerous U.S. locations. Several bus companies run routes to Seattle from adjacent cities, including BoltBus, Megabus, and FlixBus. In Seattle, bus stops are frequently found in or close to the city center, making it simple to use the city's public transportation system or to rent a car.

From Ferry

Taking a ferry to Seattle from adjacent islands or coastal towns might be an interesting and beautiful way to get there. The largest ferry company in the country, Washington State Ferries, runs several routes connecting Seattle with different Puget Sound islands, including Bainbridge Island, Vashon Island, and the San Juan Islands. Seattle's ferry terminals are close to the water and are reachable by automobile or public transportation.

Seattle is a dynamic city with a variety of transportation choices to accommodate all tastes and price ranges. Planning your vacation can make sure that your trip to the Emerald City is easy and pleasurable, regardless of whether you decide to fly, take a train, drive, ride a bus, or board a ferry. Seattle is a place worth visiting because of its breathtaking beauty, vibrant culture, and distinctive attractions, and the trip there may be an adventure in and of itself.

Seattle's top locations

The booming metropolis of Seattle, Washington, also referred to as the Emerald City is situated in the American Pacific Northwest. Seattle is a well-liked tourist destination because of its rich cultural legacy, breathtaking natural beauty, and vibrant tech environment. Finding the ideal lodging is essential to making sure your trip to this famous city is enjoyable. Here are a few of the top hotels in Seattle for visitors.

Downtown Seattle is the place to go if you want to be in the center of the activity. Many of the city's most well-known attractions can be found here, including the Space Needle, Pike Place Market, and the busy waterfront. There are several hotels in Downtown Seattle, from opulent five-star establishments to affordable choices. The benefit of staying downtown is that many of Seattle's top attractions, as well as eateries, shopping, and entertainment venues, are accessible on foot.

Capitol Hill is a wonderful option if you're searching for a hip and diverse neighborhood to stay in. Capitol Hill is well-known for its LGBTQ+ community, fashionable stores, hipster coffee shops, and exciting nightlife. It is also known for its diverse and lively culture. For those seeking a more alternative and artistic experience, Capitol Hill offers a wide selection of distinctive and boutique hotels, hostels, and vacation rentals.

Ballard: A lovely area in the city's northwest recognized for its Scandinavian and maritime history is Ballard. In addition to the renowned

Ballard Locks and Golden Gardens Park, the region is home to hip eateries, shops, and craft brewers. In contrast to downtown Seattle, Ballard has several lodging options, including hotels and vacation homes.

South Lake Union: South Lake Union is the place to be if you're interested in Seattle's burgeoning tech culture. Both the scenic Lake Union waterfront and the corporate headquarters of tech behemoths like Amazon and Google are located in this area. For business travelers or those seeking a slick and modern experience, South Lake Union offers a mix of upmarket hotels and contemporary vacation apartments.

Belltown: Belltown, which is a trendy and energetic district just north of downtown Seattle, is well-known for its strong arts and music scene. Belltown is a well-liked destination for young travelers and those seeking a vibrant and active atmosphere thanks to its abundance of art galleries, live music venues, and fashionable bars. In Belltown, there are many boutique hotels and vacation homes that offer a blend of contemporary conveniences and distinctive character.

Queen Anne: Queen Anne is an excellent choice if you're searching for a more affluent residential area to stay in. Queen Anne provides a delightful and opulent experience and is well known for its stunning historic mansions, tree-lined lanes, and expansive vistas of the city. There are various boutique hotels and vacation homes in the neighborhood, which provide a calm and elegant atmosphere.

Pioneer Square is an area that history buffs should not miss. The district, which is renowned for its gorgeous brick houses, cobblestone streets, and ancient architecture, is where Seattle's original immigrants landed in the 1850s. Pioneer Square's plethora of art galleries, antique stores, and underground tours provide a distinctive and nostalgic experience. In Pioneer Square, there are several boutique hotels and vacation homes that combine old-world beauty with contemporary comforts.

In conclusion, Seattle provides a wide selection of neighborhoods and lodging options to accommodate various tastes and price ranges. There is something for everyone, from the busy downtown to hip areas like Capitol Hill and Ballard to more expensive choices like Queen Anne.

Moving around via public transport

Exploring Seattle: Using Public Transportation to Get Around the Emerald City

Seattle, also referred to as the "Emerald City," is a bustling and exciting tourist destination. This gem of the Pacific Northwest offers something for everyone to enjoy, from the recognizable Space Needle to the busy Pike Place Market. The effective and easily available public transit system in Seattle is one of the greatest ways to travel and take advantage of everything the city has to offer. We'll look at how a tourist can successfully use public transportation in Seattle in this article.

King County Metro manages Seattle's public transportation network, which consists of buses, light rail, and streetcars. Seattle has an extensive network that makes it simple and economical to travel throughout the city and its environs. Here are some pointers to help visitors get around Seattle on public transportation.

Plan Your Route: It's important to plan your route before beginning your Seattle journey. You can enter your starting location and destination on the King County Metro website to find the most efficient bus or light rail route. You may also download a variety of transportation applications, like OneBusAway or transportation, which offer real-time arrival information, maps, and schedules and make it simple to plan your route while on the move.

Purchase an ORCA Card. The ORCA card is a reusable, contactless smart card that enables you to pay for fares on some public transportation systems in the Puget Sound area, including King County Metro, Sound Transit, and the Washington State Ferries. ORCA cards are available for purchase online, at retail locations, and in transit hubs. In comparison to buying with cash or a paper ticket, they offer a lower fare, and they are simple to reload with money for future use.

Take the Light Rail: Link, the city's light rail system, is a quick and dependable method to get around Seattle. The Red Line and Blue Line, its two current lines, link the city's center to the University of Washington, the airport, and some communities. The light rail is a great choice for longer trips or avoiding traffic jams because it runs regularly, with trains coming every 6 to 15 minutes during peak hours.

Take a Bus: Seattle and the neighboring areas are served by a massive bus network run by King County Metro. Buses are an easy way to travel to areas, points of interest, and places that the light rail may not be able to reach. Since most buses have bike racks, it is simple to combine biking and public transportation for a multi-modal excursion. Depending on the route and the time of day, buses operate at varied frequencies. Use the Seattle Streetcar: The South Lake Union Line and the First Hill Line are two of Seattle's streetcar lines, which offer a distinctive way to see the city. The streetcars connect important neighborhoods like South Lake Union, Capitol Hill, and Pioneer Square and operate on specially designated lines. They provide a nostalgic and charming way to visit the city's landmarks and run often during peak hours.

Consider taking the Waterfront Streetcar, also known as the George Benson Waterfront Streetcar Line, for a beautiful journey along Seattle's waterfront. The Great Wheel, the Olympic Sculpture Park, and the Seattle Aquarium are just a few of the sights along the waterfront that may be seen while riding this classic streetcar that runs on an old track.

Peak Hours and Fare Payment: It's crucial to be aware of peak hours when using Seattle's public transit, which is often during the morning and evening rush hours on weekdays. Buses and trains might be busier and take longer to move during certain times. Make sure you have a valid form of payment for your fare, such as an ORCA card or cash.

Average cost of boarding a train in Seattle

In the picturesque Pacific Northwest region of the United States, Seattle offers some options for boarding trains, making it easy and pleasurable to travel by train. Understanding the typical cost of taking a train in Seattle is crucial for planning and budgeting your travel expenses, whether you're taking a short trip or a longer one.

Amtrak, the country's largest rail carrier for passengers, runs many train routes that go through Seattle. The Amtrak Cascades is the most well-liked route; it travels from Eugene, Oregon to Vancouver, British Columbia, Canada, stopping in Seattle, Tacoma, and other cities en route. The Amtrak Cascades is renowned for its beautiful vistas of the coast of the Pacific Northwest and its spacious, contemporary trains. Several variables, such as the type of ticket, the level of service, the location, and the time of travel, affect the cost of using a train in Seattle.

There are three service tiers available on the Amtrak Cascades: Business Class, First Class, and Standard Class. First Class offers extra benefits including meals, alcoholic beverages, and access to the First Class club at specific stations, while Business Class gives conveniences like priority boarding, assigned seating, and free non-alcoholic beverages.

By 2023, a one-way ticket in Standard Class on the Amtrak Cascades costs, on average, roughly $26, while those in Business Class and First Class start at, respectively, about $37 and $65, respectively. Depending on the service class and the time of travel, prices for lengthier trips, such as those from Seattle to Vancouver, British Columbia, can range from $40 to $120 or more. It's important to keep in mind that rates might change depending on demand, and they might be higher during busy travel times or for last-minute reservations.

Amtrak charges extra for extras like checked baggage, reserved seats, and Wi-Fi access in addition to the base ticket. For instance, beginning in 2023, Standard Class passengers on the Amtrak Cascades must pay $8 to book a seat, whereas First Class and Business Class passengers are free to do so. Standard Class passengers have free access to Wi-Fi, but upgraded Wi-Fi service is not free. The cost of checked bags ranges from $20 to $30 per bag, depending on the number of bags and the destination.

As rates and surcharges are subject to change, it is advised to check Amtrak's website or get in touch with their customer support for the most recent details on ticket costs and fees.

There are other trains you can board in Seattle than Amtrak. The Sounder commuter rail, for instance, is run by Sound Transit and covers the Puget Sound area, stopping at places including Tacoma, Lakewood, and Everett. The cost of taking the Sounder train varies based on the distance traveled, with one-way tickets costing anywhere between $3.25 and $5.75. Additionally, Sound Transit offers reduced rates for children, the elderly, and people with impairments.

Summarily, some variables, such as the kind of ticket, service class, destination, and potential add-ons, affect the average cost of taking a train in Seattle. As of 2023, one-way tickets on the Amtrak Cascades start at about $26 for Standard Class, while First Class and Business Class offer more luxuries at a greater cost. You should visit Amtrak's website or get in touch with their customer support to get the most recent details on ticket costs and fees. For travel inside the Puget Sound region, other train choices, such as the commuter train Sounder, also provide reasonable pricing. Making preparations in advance and being aware of the boarding expenses

Cost of hiring a car

Seattle is a thriving metropolis renowned for its breathtaking natural beauty, tech-forward lifestyle, and thriving arts scene. Renting a car might be a practical way to experience everything Emerald City has to offer, whether you're a local or a guest. To properly plan your budget, it's crucial to know the average cost of renting a car in Seattle before you go out on the road.

The price of renting a car in Seattle can change depending on several variables, including the kind of vehicle, how long the rental is, where it is, and the season. A compact or midsize sedan, which is considered to be a standard-sized automobile, will often cost you $30 to $100 each day. Luxury or specialty vehicles, however, can cost more; daily prices might range from $100 to $300 or more.

The length of the rental period affects the price significantly. With reductions for longer-term rentals, the majority of automobile rental agencies offer daily, weekly, and monthly rates. Typically, daily rates are more expensive than weekly or monthly prices. For instance, a tiny car's daily charge would be around $40, while a weekly rate might be $200 or more, yielding significant long-term savings.

The cost of renting a car in Seattle also heavily depends on location. Due to added fees and taxes, renting a car from an airport or downtown location is typically more expensive. To get the greatest deal, it's a good idea to check the costs offered by various rental companies and areas. Remember that prices can change depending on the season, with costlier times of year being major tourist seasons.

There are other fees and costs involved with renting a car in Seattle in addition to the regular rental cost. Taxes, levies, and insurance costs are a few examples. When planning your budget for a rental automobile, it's important to factor in taxes and surcharges because they can increase the whole cost by 20% or more. According to the level of coverage, rental car insurance is often given as an add-on option and can cost anywhere from $10 to $30 each day. It's crucial to thoroughly consider your insurance alternatives and decide whether you require more coverage or if your current insurance, such as that provided by your credit card or private auto insurance, is adequate.

Keeping an eye out for potential hidden expenditures is also important. Others may ask you to refuel the vehicle before returning it, or they may charge you more for petrol if you don't. Some rental car companies may charge you extra for mileage if you go over a specific threshold. To prevent any unpleasant surprises while returning the automobile, it is crucial to carefully read the rental agreement and comprehend the terms and restrictions.

Finally, it's important to think about any extra features or services you might require, such as kid safety seats, GPS navigation, or additional drivers. It's crucial to account for these extras in your budget because they can raise the entire cost of renting a car in Seattle.

The typical cost of renting a car in Seattle might vary based on the kind of vehicle, how long the rental is for, where it is, what time of year it is, and other fees and costs. A standard-sized automobile will typically cost you $30 to $100 per day, with luxury or specialty vehicles being more expensive. To accurately estimate the cost of your Seattle vehicle rental, it's important to read the rental agreement thoroughly, comprehend the terms and restrictions, and take into account any additional services or features you might require. You may obtain the greatest deal and have a pleasurable and cost-effective vehicle rental experience in Seattle by comparing prices from several rental agencies and locations and being aware of any hidden fees.

Cost of boarding a taxi

Understanding the Factors That Affect Taxi Fare: The Average Cost of Boarding a Taxi

Around the world, taxis have long been a preferred means of transportation for many people. Taxis offer a practical means to go from point A to point B, whether it's for a short journey to the airport, a trip across town, or a night out. It's crucial to comprehend the aspects that affect the cost of taking a cab, though, as with any service.

The distance traveled is one of the main aspects that determine how much a taxi ride will cost. The "metered" fare, which most taxis use to determine their prices, is based on a mix of distance and time. Based on the distance traveled, which is commonly expressed in miles or kilometers, the taxi meter determines the fare. The fare will increase as the distance increases. It's crucial to be informed of the cost structure in your area because different taxi companies may have somewhat different charges per mile or kilometer.

The hour of the day or day of the week is another element that affects taxi prices. When there is a significant demand for taxis, such as during rush hour or late at night, many taxis impose higher fees. Some taxi companies may also charge extra fees for rides booked during specified times, such as holidays or weekends; this is frequently referred to as "surge pricing" or "peak pricing." Budgeting for a taxi ride requires that you be aware of these potential costs.

The price can also vary depending on the taxi or service you select. As indicated before, traditional taxis, commonly referred to as "black cabs" in various cities, are usually metered. But there are also ride-hailing services with a distinct pricing structure, like Uber or Lyft. These services frequently employ dynamic pricing, which allows prices to change based on variables like demand, the time of day, and the route traveled. In addition, some ride-hailing services may provide multiple service levels at various price points, such as economy, premium, or luxury.

When boarding a taxi, additional fees can also be applicable. For instance, there can be additional charges for luggage, extra passengers, or tolls. If you ask the driver to wait for you somewhere or if the taxi is held up in traffic for a long time, certain taxis may also charge a waiting fee. To avoid unpleasant surprises when it comes to the final fare, it's crucial to be aware of these potential fees and to inquire about them from the taxi driver or ride-hailing service before beginning your trip.

Lastly, taxi prices may be impacted by regional laws and taxes. To support local transportation programs or infrastructure upgrades, additional taxes or surcharges may be imposed on the fee in some towns or nations. Depending on the area, these extra fees might range substantially and have a sizable impact on the overall cost of a taxi ride.

Some varies, including the distance traveled, the time of day or day of the week, the type of taxi or service used, additional fees for luggage, tolls, waiting time, and local restrictions or taxes, affect the average cost of using a taxi. When planning a budget for a taxi ride, it's critical to consider these elements and to enquire with the driver or service provider about any potential fees or surcharges. You may also plan and budget effectively by using a taxi fare estimator or calculating the price of your trip beforehand. You can make wise choices and have a clear grasp of the cost of using a cab for your next journey by being aware of the elements that affect taxi fares.

Chapter 4: Exploring Seattle

Get ready for an adventure if a trip to Seattle is on your agenda! This bustling American city on the Pacific Northwest coast is renowned for its breathtaking natural beauty, extensive cultural history, and thriving arts scene. Here are some suggestions on how a tourist might explore Seattle and make the most of their trip, from famous landmarks to undiscovered gems.

Visit the renowned Pike Place Market as the first stop on your journey. With its lively vendors selling fresh vegetables, seafood, flowers, and one-of-a-kind crafts, this ancient market is a must-see. Don't pass up the opportunity to see the entertaining fish chucking at the Pike Place Fish Market, a custom that has become a familiar sight in Seattle.

The famed Space Needle is located at the Seattle Center, so go there next. This famous building provides stunning views over the city and the mountains in the area. Ride the elevator to the top of the Space Needle to enjoy the interactive exhibits and panoramic views from the observation deck.

The Olympic National Park must be visited by everybody who appreciates nature. This UNESCO World Heritage site is only a short drive from Seattle and provides untouched wilderness, temperate rainforests, and breathtaking alpine meadows. In this magnificent park, hiking, camping, and wildlife watching are all very popular activities.

Visit the Museum of Pop Culture (MoPOP), which is housed at the Seattle Center, to fully immerse yourself in Seattle's vibrant cultural environment. This one-of-a-kind museum highlights the fusion of pop culture, music, science fiction, and other topics. MoPOP provides an interesting and immersive experience for visitors of all ages, from the classic exhibits on Nirvana and Jimi Hendrix to the interactive sci-fi and fantasy displays.

Visit Capitol Hill to get a sense of Seattle's thriving arts community. Capitol Hill is a hub of culture and is known for its hip stores, unique eateries, and bright street art. Visit nearby art galleries, see a live music performance at one of the many venues, or just take a stroll through the neighborhood to take in the creative vibe.

Without partaking in Seattle's renowned coffee culture, no trip there would be complete. To experience the rich flavors of locally roasted beans, visit the original Starbucks at Pike Place Market or browse the city's countless small coffee shops.

Seattle is a city that offers everything for everyone, to sum up. There are many ways to discover and take in the finest of what Seattle has to offer, regardless of whether you enjoy the outdoors, history, or art. This dynamic city will enthrall you with its distinctive fusion of natural beauty, culture, and creativity, from recognizable landmarks to undiscovered treasures. So prepare for a memorable trip to Emerald City by packing your bags!

Top Seattle's restaurants

The Emerald City, or Seattle, is a bustling culinary destination that provides a wide variety of distinctive and varied dining experiences. There are many outstanding restaurants in Seattle to try, whether you're a local or a visitor. Here are five Seattle eateries that are a must-visit for tourists, from seafood to farm-to-table fare.

Canlis is a fine dining establishment that has been a Seattle landmark since 1950 and is renowned for its opulent ambiance, breathtaking views of Lake Union and the city skyline, and superior service. Modernized Pacific Northwest cuisine employing elements from the area is offered on the menu. Highlights of the cuisine include items like their renowned Canlis salad, wood plank grilled salmon, and wagyu beef. Canlis is a great place for a special occasion or a romantic dinner because it also has a sizable wine list.

Pike Place Chowder is a must-try for seafood fans and is housed at the renowned Pike Place Market. This quaint restaurant is well known for its award-winning chowders, which include spicy seafood chowder, creamy seafood bisque, and traditional New England clam chowder. Additionally, they offer mouthwatering crab rolls, fresh oysters, and fish & chips. Pike Place Chowder is a well-liked destination for both locals and tourists due to its relaxed atmosphere and mouthwatering seafood.

The Walrus and the Carpenter is a hip oyster bar in the Ballard district that is well-known for its delicious seafood and cozy setting. Oysters from the Pacific Northwest and beyond are available on the menu, along with other delectable small plates including grilled sardines, marinated mussels, and house-made charcuterie. This place is well-liked for happy hour or a laid-back night out because of the remarkable craft beers and cocktails.

Sitka & Spruce is a farm-to-table restaurant with a focus on locally produced, seasonally appropriate products. It is situated on Capitol Hill. The menu is constantly changing to highlight the freshest ingredients, but you can anticipate dishes like roasted meats, house-made kinds of pasta, and vegetables that have been wood-fired. An exceptional eating experience is created by the quaint, minimalist setting with an open kitchen, as well as the great attention to detail in the food and service.

Shiro's Sushi - Shiro's Sushi is one of the best places in Seattle to find genuine Japanese sushi. Seattle is known for its great sushi. This modest, unassuming restaurant in Belltown offers an omakase experience with the freshest fish flown in from all over the world and is run by expert sushi chef Shiro Kashiba, who was the original sushi chef at the well-known Shiro's in Belltown. Sushi lovers must visit Shiro's because of the unrivaled quality and workmanship of its sushi.

Following the title of one of renowned chef M.F.K. Fisher's books, this little neighborhood eatery in Queen Anne serves rustic Italian food with a contemporary touch. The menu offers items like wood-fired pizzas, homemade kinds of pasta, and braised meats that are all prepared with ingredients that are acquired locally. How to Cook a Wolf is a well-liked location for a relaxed meal or weekend brunch because of the cozy atmosphere, welcoming staff, and delectable food.

Lark is a farm-to-table restaurant with a Capitol Hill location that is renowned for its inventive drinks and small foods with a Mediterranean influence. With seasonal, locally sourced ingredients, the menu offers delicacies including wood-fired flatbreads, roasted veggies, and grilled meats. It's a terrific place for a night out with friends because of the chic, modern decor, the open kitchen, the vast wine list, and the craft cocktails.

Top Seattle's cussines

Delicious Delights: A Look at the Best Cuisines in Seattle

The dynamic and diversified city of Seattle, Washington, is well-known for its burgeoning culinary scene. For foodies, Seattle provides a wide range of culinary experiences, from farm-to-table fare to fresh seafood. Here, we'll examine the best cuisines Seattle has to offer, from time-honored classics to cutting-edge dishes that celebrate the city's distinctive culinary tradition.

Wholesome seafood

Seattle is known for its succulent seafood because it is a seaside city. For seafood lovers, a must-visit location is the well-known Pike Place Market, which is situated in the center of downtown Seattle. Many seafood sellers selling a variety of fish, crab, shrimp, and other seafood can be found in the market. Don't skip the renowned Pike Place Fish Market, where you may enjoy the audience's entertainment by watching the fishmongers toss fish to each other deftly.

Seattle is also well-known for its delectable clam chowder, which is offered at a wide variety of eateries in thick, satisfying bowls. Ivar's Acres of Clams, a Seattle landmark that has been selling seafood since 1938, is one well-liked location.

Farm-to-Table:

Seattle has a booming farm-to-table scene, with many eateries emphasizing seasonal, sustainable food and sourcing their supplies locally. Through their expertly made cuisine, these establishments place a strong emphasis on displaying the regional natural flavors of the Pacific Northwest. For instance, the trendy Ballard neighborhood restaurant The Walrus and the Carpenter is renowned for its delectable and inventive use of fresh oysters and locally sourced ingredients.

Fusion Asian:

The diverse population of Seattle has helped to create a thriving Asian fusion culinary scene. Many restaurants combine classic Asian flavors with contemporary culinary techniques, from Japanese to Vietnamese to Thai. Momiji, a renowned restaurant on Capitol Hill, serves up modernized Japanese fare that includes special toppings like foie gras and truffle oil on meals like sushi rolls.

Artisanal breweries

Seattle is frequently referred to as the "Craft Beer Capital of the World," and it is not to be missed if you enjoy craft beer. Numerous brewpubs and microbreweries in the city serve a wide selection of distinctive and mouthwatering beers. Popular local brewery Fremont Brewing is situated in the Fremont district and is well-known for its award-winning IPAs and seasonal brews.

Culture of Coffee:
Seattle is renowned for its coffee culture as well; it is the origin of Starbucks and has a large number of independent coffee shops that are popular with both locals and visitors. Seattle is a sanctuary for coffee lovers since so many coffee shops there roast their beans and provide a wide range of brewing techniques. Victrola Coffee Roasters, a well-liked location on Capitol Hill, is renowned for its superior coffee and welcoming ambiance.

Food from the Pacific Northwest:
As a result of Seattle's location in the Pacific Northwest, many restaurants serve food that emphasizes the fresh produce, seafood, and foraged delicacies found there. The greatest of

Pacific Northwest cuisine is included on the tasting menu at Canlis, a renowned fine dining establishment in Seattle. Dishes on the menu include cedar-smoked king salmon and wild mushroom risotto.

In conclusion, Seattle's culinary scene is a fusion of tastes, offering a wide variety of cuisines to suit all tastes. Whatever your culinary preferences, Seattle has something to offer, whether you enjoy seafood, farm-to-table fare, Asian fusion, craft beer, fine coffee, or simply Northwest cuisine. Seattle is undoubtedly a food lover's heaven because of its creative chefs, focus on local and sustainable foods and distinctive culinary traditions.

Seattle's street foods

Food lovers can indulge in a wide variety of gastronomic delights in Seattle, which is known for its thriving food culture. Street food is one of the many culinary options that is particularly beloved by both locals and visitors. The street food culture in Seattle is a fusion of flavors, with a wide variety of cuisines and distinctive food trucks serving up mouthwatering and creative dishes. Here, we look at some of Seattle's best street meals that are sure to tempt your palate.

Pike Place Market Chowder is a must-visit location for seafood enthusiasts and is situated inside the renowned Pike Place Market. A popular Seattle tradition, their clam chowder is creamy, award-winning, created with ingredients obtained locally, and served in a sourdough bread bowl. For a chilly day in the city, the hefty servings and rich tastes make it the ideal comfort food choice.

Look no further than Marination Mobile if you're in the mood for some delectable Hawaiian-Korean fusion food. The exquisite menu at this well-known food truck has dishes like their signature Kalua Pork Sliders, Spicy Pork Tacos, and Kimchi Rice Bowl. The legendary Nunya Sauce and the sweet and savory flavors make for a genuinely distinctive and mouthwatering dining experience.

Maximus Minimus: Maximus Minimus is a must-try for all BBQ enthusiasts out there. With its eye-catching pig-shaped appearance, this unusual food truck is difficult to overlook. They specialize in toasted pulled pork sandwiches with coleslaw and your choice of "Maximus" (spicy) or "Minimus" (mild) sauce. You'll be begging for more because of the winning combination of the acidic sauce and the soft, smokey pork. Food truck Nosh: Craving some premium hot dogs? Nosh Food Truck is the only place to go. This well-liked food truck provides inventive toppings and flavor combinations on traditional hot dogs. Nosh Food Truck challenges what a hot dog can be, from the Truffle Mac & Cheese Dog to the PB&J Dog with bacon jam, providing hot dog lovers with a unique and delectable experience.

BeanFish: This food truck serves authentic Japanese taiyaki, making it a must-stop for those with a sweet craving. A fish-shaped waffle called a taiyaki can be filled with either sweet or savory ingredients, and BeanFish offers a delicious selection of flavors like Nutella, custard, and red bean. These tasty sweets are the ideal quick dessert or on-the-go snack because they are warm and crispy.

Off the Rez: Celebrating Native American cuisine, the Off the Rez food truck offers mouthwatering concoctions of vintage and contemporary tastes. Their cuisine offers a distinctive and gratifying dining experience, with dishes ranging from bison burgers with huckleberry sauce to Indian tacos with fry bread. Off the Rez stands apart in Seattle's street food scene because it incorporates Native American culinary traditions and uses locally sourced, organic products.

Skillet Street Food: Known for its gourmet burgers and poutine, Skillet Street Food is a famous food truck in Seattle. A favorite among customers is their Bacon Jam Burger, which is constructed with grass-fed beef, arugula, blue cheese, and their house-made bacon jam. Additionally, their poutine, which consists of crispy fries covered in gravy and cheese curds, is a warming treat that will satiate your hunger.

The street food scene in Seattle is a foodie's dream come true, delivering a wide variety of tastes and gastronomic adventures. Everything from rich chowders to savory BBQ, exquisite hot dogs to sweet taiyaki, and inventive fusion food to Native American delicacies.

In Seattle, are there any dietary restrictions?
People with dietary restrictions can discover a wide variety of options in Seattle, a city noted for its thriving food industry. Seattle's culinary scene has developed to meet the specific needs of its diverse population, which includes people with a range of dietary choices, allergies, intolerances, and medical issues. Seattle boasts a bustling food scene that can accommodate a wide range of dietary requirements, from

vegetarian and vegan diets to gluten-free, dairy-free, and nut-free options.

Vegetarianism and veganism are two of the most prevalent dietary restrictions. Numerous plant-based restaurants in Seattle serve scrumptious and healthy dishes made completely of plant-based components. Capitol Hill's "Plum Bistro," one of the city's most well-liked vegan restaurants, serves a varied menu of vegan comfort cuisine, featuring dishes like vegan mac & cheese, crunchy tofu nuggets, and savory vegetable stir-fries. "Veggie Grill," a fast-casual brand that offers mouthwatering plant-based burgers, bowls, and salads, is another well-known vegan eatery in Seattle.

Seattle has a large gluten-free population, and many restaurants have gluten-free menus or even completely gluten-free selections. Pizza fans who avoid gluten adore "Razzi's Pizzeria," which is situated in Greenwood. For customers with celiac illness or gluten intolerance, they provide a special gluten-free kitchen and a large assortment of gluten-free toppings, crusts, and sauces. Another well-known gluten-free establishment in Seattle is "Capitol Cider," which is situated on Capitol Hill and serves a wide variety of gluten-free ciders as well as a gluten-free menu that includes things like cider-braised pork tacos and cider-battered fish and chips.

Seattle offers a wide variety of dairy-free options as well for people who have dairy allergies or lactose intolerance. A range of dairy-free ice cream flavors is available at "Frankie & Jo's," an artisanal plant-based ice cream shop, which uses healthy ingredients including coconut milk and cashew milk. Many dairy-free options, such as smoothie bowls, sandwiches, and salads made with plant-based cheese and milk substitutes, are available on the menu at "Chaco Canyon Organic Café," which has multiple locations in Seattle.

Seattle offers nut-free options or has nut-free kitchens, so it also accommodates people with nut allergies. "Cafe Flora," a well-known vegetarian and vegan eatery in Madison Valley, has a nut-free kitchen and serves a range of nut-free dishes, including their well-known mushroom Wellington and an almond butter and jelly sandwich made with sunflower seed butter. Another well-known nut-free restaurant is "Portage Bay Cafe," which has several locations in Seattle. It offers a special nut-free menu for people with allergies that includes things like nut-free pancakes and waffles.

Seattle offers a wide variety of markets and grocery stores that can accommodate particular dietary needs in addition to its specialty dining establishments. "PCC Community Markets," a neighborhood co-op supermarket chain, provides a large selection of organic, regionally produced, and specialty goods, as well as a range of gluten-free, dairy-free, and vegan options. Another well-known grocery shop in Seattle, "Central Co-op," sells a wide variety of foods for people with dietary restrictions, such as organic vegetables, gluten-free snacks, and dairy-free substitutes.

Seattle is a city that respects and offers a wide variety of options for people with dietary requirements. There are several eateries and grocery stores in Seattle that offer a variety of dietary demands, from vegan and gluten-free to dairy-free and nut-free. If you have a particular dietary choice, allergy, intolerance, or medical condition, you can still enjoy delectable meals in Emerald City without having to sacrifice your nutritional needs. Seattle's food culture is always changing to suit the need

Finding low-cost lodging in Seattle

Seattle is a well-liked tourist destination in the United States thanks to its scenic surroundings, recognizable attractions, and dynamic culture. However, it might be difficult to locate reasonable lodging in this busy city because of the high cost of living there. But don't worry! Visitors to Seattle can discover affordable lodging that won't break the bank with some careful planning and research. Here are some suggestions for finding inexpensive lodging in Seattle.

Choose Budget Hotels or Motels: While there are many luxurious hotels in Seattle, there are also several affordable options. If you're ready to stay a little beyond the city center, many motels and discount hotels offer affordable rates. Options in commuter-friendly communities like North Seattle, South Seattle, and Tacoma typically cost less. These affordable lodging options frequently include standard facilities like free Wi-Fi, breakfast, and spotless rooms, making them an economical choice for travelers on a tight budget.

Think about Hostels: Hostels are a great choice for travelers on a budget. Numerous hostels in Seattle provide inexpensive dormitory-style lodging where you can share a room with other tourists. Hostels are fantastic places to meet other travelers and share travel advice and tales.

Private rooms, which might be more reasonably priced for couples or small groups, are also available in several hostels in Seattle.

Look for Airbnb rentals: If you're looking for cheap lodging in Seattle, Airbnb is a well-liked choice. Locals frequently use Airbnb to rent out extra rooms, flats, or even entire houses, providing affordable alternatives to regular hotels. There are several possibilities available, ranging from comfortable rooms in shared homes to complete apartments with kitchens, providing you the freedom to prepare your meals and reduce your heating bills. To ensure a pleasant visit, just remember to read reviews, check the area, and get in touch with the host.

Investigate Extended Stay Hotels: For visitors considering a longer stay in Seattle, extended stay hotels or serviced apartments can be an affordable choice. These lodgings are less expensive than regular hotels since they provide amenities like kitchens and laundry rooms, as well as frequently having weekly or monthly prices. Although extended-stay hotels are frequently found in suburbs, they provide quick access to public transportation for city exploration.

Investigate Discounts and bargains: Seattle offers several tourist discounts and bargains that might help you save money on lodging. For instance, some hotels provide lower rates for reservations made in advance or during the off-peak season. Furthermore, companies like Expedia, Booking.com, or Hotels.com frequently offer package discounts or reduced rates on lodging. Find the greatest offers that meet your budget by doing some research and comparing rates.

Think about camping or RV parks: If you enjoy the outdoors, lodging at an RV park or while camping can be an interesting and inexpensive choice in Seattle. Many campgrounds and RV parks in and around the city provide beautiful views and outdoor adventures. But be aware that certain campgrounds and RV parks may have few amenities, so be ready for a more basic experience.

In conclusion, even though Seattle is renowned for having higher living expenses, travelers can still find inexpensive housing options. You may locate affordable lodgings in Seattle without sacrificing comfort and security by taking into account bargain hotels or motels, hostels, Airbnb rentals, extended stay hotels, researching discounts and offers, or even camping or staying at RV parks. You can spend less on lodging and more on discovering the Emerald City's splendor with careful planning and study. Travel safely!

Top Seattle shopping malls

NSeattle, which is renowned for its thriving culture, extensive history, and breathtaking natural beauty, is also a shopping paradise. This thriving city in the Pacific Northwest offers a wide variety of shopping possibilities for locals and visitors alike, from hip boutiques to regional markets. In this post, we'll look at Seattle's greatest shopping districts where you can indulge in retail therapy and find one-of-a-kind items.

Pike Place Market is a renowned location for shoppers and is situated in the center of downtown Seattle. One of the oldest continually operating public markets in the United States, this historic market has been open since 1907. There are a ton of stalls here that sell local seafood, unique arts and crafts, and vintage items in addition to fresh veggies. Don't forget to see the colorful "fish throwing" competition between the fishmongers at the Pike Place Fish Market, which is renowned worldwide. A trip to Pike Place Market is essential for experiencing real Seattle shopping.

Seattle Premium Outlets: If you enjoy shopping for designer items at reduced costs, this is the place for you. This outdoor outlet mall, which is roughly 30 miles north of downtown Seattle, has over 120 stores and offers affordable designer names including Coach, Michael Kors, Kate Spade, and Nike. Seattle Premium Outlets is a well-liked shopping destination for both locals and tourists due to its lovely surroundings and variety of retailers.

University Village is an upscale shopping mall located in Seattle's University District that is renowned for its open-air design and chic retailers. A variety of local and national boutiques selling clothing, accessories, home goods, and other items may be found here. A leisurely day of shopping and dining is ideal at the attractively manicured outdoor mall, which also offers a range of food alternatives.

Capitol Hill: Capitol Hill is a hip district in Seattle that provides a one-of-a-kind shopping experience and is known for its hipster ambiance and unusual boutiques. Capitol Hill is a treasure trove for people looking for unusual and diverse finds, with everything from vintage clothing shops to independent bookshops, record stores, and art galleries. Capitol Hill is a diverse and welcoming retail district since it has a wide variety of LGBTQ+-friendly stores and boutiques.

Westlake Center is a multi-level shopping center with a variety of shops that are situated in the center of downtown Seattle. Westlake Center offers a wide variety of goods for any customer, from upscale clothing labels to well-known department stores like Nordstrom and Macy's. The mall is a well-liked shopping destination for both locals and tourists since it has a wide selection of culinary establishments and conducts special events and activities throughout the year. As the "Center of the Universe," Seattle's Fremont area is eccentric and bohemian and provides a distinctive retail experience. A wide variety of boutiques, vintage shops, and creative stores can be found here, selling everything from handcrafted goods to vintage apparel, antiques, and one-of-a-kind presents. The well-known Fremont Sunday Market, a lively street market with a unique selection of regional produce, handcrafted goods, and street cuisine, is also located in Fremont.

Ballard: A picturesque Seattle area noted for its maritime history and up-and-coming stores, Ballard is situated along the waterfront. A variety of boutiques, home décor shops, and art galleries may be found here. Ballard is renowned for having a Scandinavian heritage, and many of its businesses sell distinctive presents and other products with a Nordic flair. Don't miss the Ballard Farmers Market, which sells wonderful street cuisine, fresh veggies, and regional crafts.

Seattle's Top beaches

The Best Beaches in Seattle: A Haven for Nature Lovers

Seattle, a thriving metropolis in the Pacific Northwest, is renowned for its distinctive skyline, top-notch cuisine, and extensive cultural history. Beyond the city's urban setting, however, is a treasure trove of breathtaking beaches that provide a tranquil haven for beachgoers and nature lovers both. Here are the greatest beaches in Seattle that are worth visiting, which range from long lengths of sand to rocky shorelines.

Alki Beach is a Seattle institution.
Alki Beach in West Seattle is a typical Seattle beach that provides sweeping views of the Olympic Mountains and the metropolitan skyline. This area of sand is well-liked for beach volleyball, swimming, and sunbathing. Along the paved promenade that runs along to the shore, it's also a nice area for a stroll or bike ride. With its numerous picnic tables and fire pits, the beach is the ideal location for a beach bonfire and a BBQ with friends and family. Don't miss the chance to visit the Alki Point Lighthouse, which has been directing ships into Puget Sound since 1913, if you're a history lover.

Beach and park combined at Golden Gardens Park
The Ballard neighborhood's Golden Gardens Park is a well-liked hangout for both beachgoers and outdoor aficionados. This large park is the ideal place for an outdoor activity-filled day

because it has a sandy beach, hiking paths, picnic spaces, and a boat launch. The beach is a popular location for watching sunsets and is renowned for its stunning views of the Olympic Mountains and Puget Sound. At low tide, you may stroll through tidal pools teaming with marine life or just unwind on the sand and take in the surrounding splendor.

A Paradise for Nature Lovers, Discovery Park Beach

The largest city park in Seattle, Discovery Park, is situated in Magnolia and offers a distinctive fusion of the outdoors with a rich past. Miles of hiking trails wind through forests, meadows, and sea cliffs in this park, offering breathtaking vistas of the Olympic Mountains and Puget Sound. The Discovery Park Beach is located in the center of the park; it is a quiet section of the coastline ideal for beachcombing, birdwatching, and admiring the tranquil beauty of the surrounding landscape. The beach is well-known for its shoreline littered with driftwood and provides a tranquil haven from the bustle of city life.

An Undiscovered Gem: Carkeek Park Beach
Carkeek Park, tucked away in the Broadview district of North Seattle, is a hidden gem that provides a combination of outdoor recreation and scenic beauty. The park's beach is the main attraction, although it also has hiking paths, picnic spaces, a playground, and a salmon hatchery. The Carkeek Park Beach is a remote and rocky section of coastline ideal for beachcombing, tidal pool exploration, and admiring breathtaking vistas of the Olympic Mountains and Puget Sound. You might even see fish swimming upstream in Pipers Creek, which flows through the park, during the salmon spawning season (November to December).

Beach at Lincoln Park: A Natural Playground
Families and wildlife enthusiasts alike enjoy visiting Lincoln Park in the West Seattle community of Fauntleroy. Although the park has playgrounds, hot saltwater pools, picnic spots,

and hiking routes, its beach is the real draw. The sandy Lincoln Park Beach is the ideal location for swimming, beachcombing, and taking in the breathtaking vistas of the Olympic Mountains and Puget Sound. The beach also has a distinctive feature known as "Colman Pool," a rocky outcropping that creates a swimming pool-like environment.

Seattle weekend activities

The vibrant and multicultural metropolis of Seattle also referred to as the "Emerald City," is situated in the American Pacific Northwest. With its breathtaking natural beauty, extensive history, and distinctive cultural scene, Seattle offers visitors a wide range of fun activities to take part in during weekend getaways. Every traveler may find something to enjoy in Seattle, whether they are an outdoor enthusiast, a foodie, or a history lover.

Discover Pike Place Market: Located in the center of Seattle, Pike Place Market is a renowned, busy market. Every tourist should visit this old market. Pike Place Market provides a typical Seattle experience with its unusual mix of fresh seafood, local produce, handmade goods, and street performers. Don't miss the chance to witness the renowned fish toss at the Pike Place Fish Market or to taste freshly roasted coffee at the first Starbucks location.

Visit the Space Needle: A journey to Seattle's recognizable Space Needle is a must for all tourists. Built for the 1962 World's Fair, this renowned observation tower provides sweeping views of the city, the nearby mountains, and Puget Sound. Travel to the top and dine at the rotating SkyCity restaurant for a special dining experience or take in the breathtaking views from the observation deck.

Take a stroll along the waterfront: The waterfront in Seattle is a lively, beautiful location that has several activities. Enjoy the breathtaking views of Elliott Bay, the downtown skyline, and the Olympic Mountains by taking a stroll along the waterfront. To discover more about the marine life in the area, check out the Seattle Aquarium, or board a ferry for a charming trip to one of the surrounding islands, such as Bainbridge Island or Blake Island.

Investigate the Museum Scene: Several museums in Seattle cater to a wide range of interests. History buffs can explore the Museum of History and Industry (MOHAI), which highlights the city's rich history and cultural legacy, while art fans can check out the Seattle Art Museum, which houses an excellent collection of modern and contemporary art. The Museum of Flight, which has a sizable collection of aircraft and interactive exhibitions, is a must-visit destination for aviation aficionados.

Discover the Outdoors: There are a variety of outdoor activities to choose from in the breathtaking natural splendor that surrounds Seattle. Take a walk in the adjacent Olympic National Park, which is renowned for its scenic coastline, rocky mountains, and lush rainforests. Admire Mount Rainier, an active volcano and the highest point in Washington state, when you visit Mount Rainier, National Park. Visit one of the many parks in the city, such as Gas Works Park, Discovery Park, or Green Lake Park, for a more urban outdoor experience. These parks offer lovely paths, views of the water, and recreational opportunities.

Enjoy Culinary Delights: The eclectic culinary scene in Seattle is recognized for offering a fusion of tastes from around the world. Explore the historic Pioneer Square for its quaint pubs and bistros, or visit the fashionable Capitol Hill district for its hipster cafes and contemporary eateries. Don't pass up the chance to try some of the city's well-known seafood dishes, like clam chowder, salmon, and fresh oysters. Take a food tour for a special gourmet experience to find the city's hidden food gems and learn about its culinary heritage.

Enjoy Live Performances: Seattle has a robust music and performing arts scene, with several venues and theaters that provide live performances all year long. You can see a live performance in the venerable Moore Theatre or the Showbox, or you can visit the famous Paramount Theatre, which presents Broadway plays and musicals. For fans of independent music, check out the local scene in areas like Ballard or Capitol Hill, where you can see live concerts by emerging artists in small settings.

Skydiving in Seattle

Seattle Skydiving: An Exciting Tourist Adventure

Seattle, also known as the Emerald City, is well-known for its coffee culture, the iconic Space Needle, and its thriving music scene. It also provides travelers who are adrenaline junkies with an amazing skydiving experience. Many thrill-seekers put skydiving in Seattle on their bucket lists because it offers breathtaking vistas over the Puget Sound, Mount Rainier, and the beautiful city skyline.

It's important to be prepared for this exhilarating event and understand how to get the most out of your skydiving in Seattle.

Selecting a Skydiving Facility

Selecting a trustworthy skydiving facility in Seattle is the first step in organizing your skydiving excursion. There are numerous choices, each with unique packages and services. Choose a facility that has received United States Parachute Association (USPA) accreditation, which guarantees skydivers receive training that meets industry standards for safety. To select the best option for your budget and tastes, read reviews, visit their website, and compare rates.

Organizing Your Skydive

It's time to make your skydive reservation after selecting a skydiving facility. You may reserve your space in advance at the majority of locations thanks to online booking. Be ready for potential rescheduling because weather conditions can impact skydiving operations. Before going to the drop zone, it's a good idea to check the weather forecast and call the skydiving center for any updates.

Security First

Safety comes first when skydiving. When you get to the skydiving facility, knowledgeable instructors will give you a complete safety briefing and instruction. They will go over the necessary tools, methods, and procedures to make skydiving both safe and entertaining. Pay close attention to the directions, and if anything is unclear, ask questions.

The Leap

You have the choice to partake in a tandem skydive while visiting Seattle, which is the most well-liked and secure approach for newbies to feel the rush of skydiving. When you partake in a tandem skydive, you will be attached to a skilled instructor who will handle all the technical details of the jump while you focus entirely on having fun.

After getting ready, you board the aircraft and fly up to the jump altitude, which is normally between 10,000 and 15,000 feet. Enjoy the beautiful vistas of the Pacific Northwest region below as you soar through the air. When the moment comes to jump, you will be safely fastened to your instructor and will experience an exhilarating 45 to 60-second freefall at up to 120 mph. Unbearable is the sensation of falling through the air freely; it is an experience that will stay with you forever.

Your instructor will open the parachute after the freefall, and you will then experience a tranquil and beautiful canopy ride for a while, soaking in the expansive views of the surroundings. Even a peaceful landing back at the drop zone with the chance to maneuver the parachute is possible.

Grab the Moment

The majority of skydiving facilities offer photo and video packages so you may document your experience. A professional videographer is often included in these packages, who will leap alongside you and record your whole experience, from the buildup to the jump to the freefall and the canopy ride. You can watch the breathtaking video again and relive the excitement of your skydiving.

Biking in Seattle

Biking in the Emerald City: A Comprehensive Guide to Exploring Seattle on Two Wheels

For bike aficionados, Seattle, which is renowned for its breathtaking natural beauty and eco-conscious culture, is a great location. Biking is a well-liked method of exploring the city and its surroundings because of the area's wide network of bike lanes, beautiful trails, and spectacular views. We will go into depth about how a visitor to Seattle can go riding, including the expected cost, in this extensive guide.

Seattle is a city that encourages bicycling.
Seattle is a bike-friendly city with a vast network of bike lanes and trails that make commuting on two wheels simple and secure. The city is renowned for having a thriving biking scene,

with a sizable population of cyclists who utilize their bikes for transportation, fun, and fitness. In addition to being a quick and environmentally friendly mode of transportation in Seattle, biking lets visitors explore the city at their own pace while taking in its distinctive neighborhoods, parks, and waterfront.

Rental bicycle options
There are numerous choices in Seattle for tourists who don't own bicycles to hire them. The city is filled with rental bike shops that offer a wide selection of bikes in various shapes, sizes, and accessories to accommodate a range of tastes and requirements. Helmets, locks, and maps are frequently included in rental shops to assist customers in navigating the city on their bikes.

The price of renting a bike in Seattle varies according to the kind of bike, how long the rental is, and any extra extras. A basic hybrid or city bike can be rented for $25–40 per day on average, with discounts for longer rentals. More specialized bikes, like mountain bikes or electric bikes, could be more expensive. It's always a good idea to inquire about individual rental shops' distinctive rates and rules.

Routes & Trails for Biking

Numerous biking routes and trails are available in Seattle, catering to riders of all experience levels and interests. The Burke-Gilman Trail, a 27-mile paved trail that winds through the city and connects to other locations including the picturesque Lake Washington and Puget Sound, is one of the most well-known trails. Along the route, the well-marked trail gives breathtaking views of the water, parks, and residences.

The 10-mile Alki Beach Trail in West Seattle, which follows the gorgeous Alki Beach, is another well-liked bike route. Along with providing options for seaside picnics and riverfront eateries, this path provides panoramic views of the Seattle cityscape.

The Seattle to Portland (STP) route is a difficult but worthwhile alternative for more seasoned cyclists. Riders travel through this 200-mile route through rural areas, quaint towns, and picturesque scenery before arriving in Portland, Oregon. The STP offers a distinctive approach to discovering the Pacific Northwest and is a well-liked event for serious cyclists.

Biking Tips and Safety
When biking in Seattle, like with any outside sport, safety must come first. Observe the following advice:

The wearing of a helmet is required by law for bicycles in Seattle. For your safety, be sure you put on a helmet that fits properly.

Observe traffic regulations: Biking in Seattle is subject to the same regulations as driving. Ride in the same direction as the traffic and obey all traffic signals.

Utilize the bike lanes: Seattle has a robust network of bike lanes; use them whenever you can. Keep an eye out for parked cars and opening doors by remaining vigilant.

Lock your bike: Since bike theft is a problem in cities, you should always lock your bike safely and securely with a strong lock while leaving it alone.

Wear bright colors and make yourself noticeable to drivers by using lights or reflectors.

Top festivals in Seattle
Seattle, a thriving and multicultural city in the Pacific Northwest of the United States, is renowned for its colorful festivals and rich cultural scene. In Seattle, several festivals highlight the city's distinctive personality and charm, including those that feature music, the arts, food, and drink. Here are a few of Seattle's most popular festivals that both residents and tourists look forward to.

Bumbershoot is a yearly three-day music and arts event that takes place over Labor Day weekend at the Seattle Center. It is one of the most well-known festivals in Seattle. Bumbershoot, which began in 1971, has developed into a festival that honors comedy, film, visual arts, music, and other genres. In addition to a wide range of food sellers, art exhibits, and interactive activities for all ages, the festival offers a diversified lineup of regional and international artists.

Seattle International Film Festival (SIFF): SIFF draws movie fans from all over the world since it is one of the biggest and most prominent film festivals in the United States. SIFF presents hundreds of films from all genres and nations every year for more than 25 days in May and June, including world premieres, documentaries, shorts, and more. For cinephiles, a festival is a must-attend event because it also features special screenings, workshops, and panel discussions with directors.

Northwest Folklife Festival: The Northwest Folklife Festival, a four-day event held over Memorial Day weekend at the Seattle Center, honors the cultural diversity of the Pacific Northwest. Live music, dance performances, arts & crafts, and food sellers from several ethnic communities in the area are all featured at the event. It's a rare chance to discover the rich cultural legacy of the Pacific Northwest and discover the customs and traditions of different towns.

Seattle Pride Parade and Festival: The Seattle Pride Parade and Festival, one of the biggest pride events in the country, is a colorful, welcoming celebration of LGBTQ+ rights and culture that takes place in June. Live music, drag shows, food trucks, and merchants are all part of the celebration as well as the parade, which showcases vibrant floats, performances, and neighborhood groups. It's a happy and energizing occasion that supports diversity, equality, and acceptance.

The greatest of the Pacific Northwest's culinary culture is showcased at Taste Washington, the largest single-region wine and food event in the country. This four-day event, which takes place in March and showcases the region's award-winning wines and farm-to-table cuisine, offers tastings from more than 200 wineries. It's a gourmet extravaganza that appeals to both foodies and wine connoisseurs.

The Fremont Solstice Parade and Fair, a distinctive and eccentric festival that takes place in June in the diverse Fremont neighborhood, celebrates creativity, community, and the start of summer. The event's highlight is the renowned Solstice Parade, in which vibrant and creative floats, costumes, and performances parade through the streets in a non-motorized parade. Live music, food trucks, artisan sellers, and numerous interactive games are also available at the fair.

Winterfest is an annual festival that celebrates the holiday season and is held in the Seattle

Center from late November to early January. The event turns the Seattle Center into a winter wonderland with its Winter Train and Village, ice skating rink, seasonal entertainment, and beautiful lighting. It's a cherished occasion for families and guests to celebrate the holiday season in a beautiful location.

Top Seattle art galleries

There are many art galleries in Seattle, a booming city with a thriving arts culture, where you may see a wide variety of contemporary, modern, and traditional works of art. Discovering the best art galleries in Seattle is a requirement whether you're a local art aficionado or a visitor to the Emerald City. Here, we've compiled a list of some of Seattle's top art galleries that are well worth seeing.

One of the most renowned and esteemed art museums in the Pacific Northwest is the Seattle Art Museum (SAM), which is situated in the heart of Seattle. SAM provides a thorough art experience with a varied collection that crosses several genres and eras. SAM contains everything, from masterpieces of modern and contemporary art to ancient Asian sculpture. The museum serves as a nexus for art lovers and culture vultures by presenting changing exhibits, special events, and educational programs.

Frye Art Museum: The Frye Art Museum, one of the city's oldest art galleries, has supported the neighborhood's creative scene for more than a century. The collection of 19th and 20th-century European and American artwork at this free-entry museum includes pieces by well-known artists like Franz von Stuck, Rosa Bonheur, and William-Adolphe Bouguereau. The museum offers a distinctive fusion of historical and modern art through its changing exhibitions, seminars, and workshops.

Chihuly Garden and Glass: If you enjoy glasswork, you must visit this gallery when you are in Seattle. This museum, which is part of the Seattle Center, features the magnificent creations of renowned glass artist Dale Chihuly. The museum has an inside exhibit where Chihuly's exquisite glass sculptures are on display, as well as a lovely outdoor garden where his captivating works are placed. For visitors, the fusion of glass art and rich vegetation offers a magical and immersive experience.

The well-known Seattle contemporary art gallery Greg Kucera Gallery is situated in the storied Pioneer Square district. The gallery exhibits work by both well-known and up-and-coming artists, showing a variety of media, including mixed media, painting, photography, and sculpture. Greg Kucera Gallery is renowned for its cutting-edge shows and diverse roster of artists, with a focus on thought-provoking and socially relevant work.

Traver Gallery: A premier place for modern glasswork, Traver Gallery has locations in Tacoma and downtown Seattle. Glass artwork in a variety of media, including blown glass, cast glass, and mixed media, created by both regional and international artists, is on display in the gallery. Pushing the limits of the material and displaying the most recent trends in modern glass, Traver Gallery is renowned for its unique and experimental approach to glass art.

Davidson Galleries: In Seattle, Davidson Galleries is a must-visit gallery if you're interested in printmaking and works on paper. This gallery, which is situated in the storied Pike Place Market, focuses on original prints like etchings, woodcuts, lithographs, and more. In addition to holding frequent exhibitions, workshops, and lectures on printmaking, Davidson Galleries represents a diverse spectrum of artists and artistic movements, from traditional to modern.

Foster/White Gallery is a reputable gallery for contemporary art in Seattle that exhibits works in a variety of media, such as glass, painting, sculpture, and photography. A variety of renowned artists from around the world and the local community are represented by the gallery. Foster/White Gallery serves as a focal point for city-dwelling fans of contemporary art by hosting frequent exhibitions, artist lectures, and special events

Obeying law and order

Seattle, Washington is a well-known tourist destination in the United States and provides visitors with a variety of attractions, including the iconic Space Needle, a thriving music scene, and a scenic waterfront. Seattle does, however, have its laws and ordinances that visitors should be aware of to ensure a safe and happy vacation. Here is detailed advice on how visitors to Seattle can follow the law.

Learn the laws of the area: Do some research and familiarize yourself with Seattle's rules and ordinances before venturing out to tour the city. Understanding the laws governing jaywalking, smoking, drinking in public, and other typical local prohibitions falls under this category. You can avoid any unneeded penalties or legal issues during your vacation by being aware of the legislation in advance.

Observe traffic regulations: Seattle has traffic regulations that visitors should follow. Use crosswalks to cross the street, obey traffic signals and signs, and drive or bike with caution in urban areas. Following the posted speed limits is crucial, as is avoiding using your phone while driving as distracted driving is prohibited in Seattle.

Despite being legal for recreational use in Washington State, marijuana is nonetheless governed by several laws and regulations. Marijuana smoking is not permitted in public areas, including streets, sidewalks, and parks. Driving while under the influence of marijuana is likewise prohibited. If you decide to use marijuana while in Seattle, do so alone or in a place that has been classified as cannabis-friendly.

Recycle and compost your waste appropriately. Seattle is renowned for its strong environmental initiatives. Use the marked recycling and compost containers that are supplied throughout the city as a responsible tourists to ensure proper waste disposal. Keep in mind that leaving trash lying around is not permitted in Seattle and that doing so could result in fines.

Respect public spaces: Seattle is home to many lovely parks, gardens, and waterfront places that are appreciated by both residents and visitors. Respect these public areas by abiding by the posted rules and regulations, which include not destroying or removing flora, not feeding wildlife, and not leaving trash. Be sure to abide by these guidelines if you smoke because many parks in Seattle have dedicated spaces for them.

Pay attention to noise regulations: Seattle has noise regulations in place to guarantee that locals and visitors may live in peace. In particular, try to keep your voice down when it's quiet, which is often after 10 p.m. to 7 a.m. Keep the volume of your music, talks, and other activities at an acceptable level when in public areas including parks and residential neighborhoods.

Respect the diversity and local culture: Seattle is a multicultural and accepting city that accepts various cultures, beliefs, and lifestyles. During your stay, it's crucial to respect and value the diversity and culture of the area. Avoid acting in a biased or insulting manner toward the regional traditions, customs, and practices. Be respectful of them.

Following the law is essential for tourists visiting Seattle if they want to be safe and have a good time. Follow traffic regulations, observe marijuana laws, dispose of waste appropriately, respect public areas, pay attention to noise legislation, and respect local variety and culture. You may travel in style while being a responsible and considerate guest to the Emerald City if you follow these simple guidelines.

Consider bringing medication

Due to its verdant surroundings and breathtaking waterfront vistas, Seattle is frequently referred to as the "Emerald City" by visitors from all over the world. Plan and carry your prescriptions with you when visiting Seattle, whether it's to see its famous attractions like the Space Needle or to explore its energetic areas like Pike Place Market. Here are several strong arguments for travelers to Seattle to think about packing their prescriptions.

Medical Emergencies Can Occur Anywhere: Despite Seattle's reputation for having a top-notch healthcare system, they can nonetheless occur while you're traveling. Having your meds on hand guarantees that you can receive essential care right away in the event of an accident or severe sickness. Instead of attempting to negotiate an unfamiliar healthcare system or locate a pharmacy that carries your exact prescription, it is always preferable to be prepared and have your medications on hand.

Maintain Your Health Routine: It's critical to continue your usual health regimen when traveling if you have a chronic disease that needs frequent medication. If you have diabetes, hypertension, or any other chronic illness, for instance, skipping doses or running out of medication could harm your health. You may continue to properly manage your condition and prevent any changes to your health routine by bringing your prescriptions with you.

Limited Access to Prescription Drugs: Despite Seattle's abundance of pharmacies and medical centers, some drugs might not be easily accessible without a valid prescription. If you run out of your prescription medication while on vacation, getting a new prescription and making an appointment with a local doctor may take some time. You can prevent any delays or challenges in getting the prescriptions you require by carrying your pills with you.

Travel-Induced Health Changes: Traveling, particularly between time zones, can affect your digestion as well as your sleep schedule and induce jet lag. These alterations can occasionally result in health problems like migraines, sleeplessness, or digestive disorders. Having your prescriptions on hand will help you properly manage these health changes brought on by travel and guarantee that you can enjoy your trip pain-free.

Avoid Language Barriers: Despite having a high level of English proficiency and being a varied and cosmopolitan city, Seattle can nevertheless present a language barrier for some visitors. It could be challenging to effectively express your needs to nearby healthcare professionals or pharmacists if you need specific medications with complicated names or dosages. By having your meds on hand, you can avoid the need for translation or interpretation and guarantee that you are taking the right medications as directed by your doctor.

Weather Variability: Seattle's weather is notoriously erratic, with regular downpours and temperature swings. Sometimes sudden changes in the weather might set off health problems like allergies, asthma, or joint pain. You can be ready to handle any weather-related health issues that may occur during your trip by carrying your prescriptions with you.

Conclusively, it is a smart idea to bring your medications with you when visiting Seattle. It guarantees that you can keep your daily health regimen, be ready for unanticipated medical crises, avoid language hurdles, and properly handle any health changes brought on by travel. To minimize loss or damage and to comply with transportation security laws, always carry your prescriptions in their original, labeled containers in your carry-on bag. Consult your doctor or another healthcare professional before your travel to make sure you have enough prescriptions and medication for the trip. You can travel worry-free and take advantage of everything Seattle has to offer by following these safety tips.

Getting Seattle first aid services

Seattle is a thriving city with a rich culture, stunning natural surroundings, and a wide range of attractions to keep visitors entertained. However, just like anywhere else, accidents do happen, so it's best to constantly be ready for them, especially if you're a visitor in the area. In this post, we'll look at how a visitor to Seattle can receive emergency first assistance.

Knowing the emergency phone numbers is one of the most important things visitors can do to make sure they can receive first assistance in Seattle. The emergency phone number in Seattle is 911. To contact the police, fire department, or medical emergency services, dial this number. It's crucial to remember that you should only call this number in the event of a true emergency. People who need emergency assistance may wait longer for assistance if this number is used for non-emergencies.

Visit one of Seattle's several urgent care facilities for more first aid options. These facilities are dispersed all around the city. These clinics can offer quick medical care for illnesses or injuries that are not life-threatening. Seattle Children's

Hospital Urgent Care, Concentra Urgent Care, and MultiCare Urgent Care are a few of the well-known urgent care facilities in Seattle. The majority of the time, these amenities are accessible seven days a week without an appointment.

Visitors may also go to one of Seattle's numerous hospitals in the event of a catastrophic injury or medical emergency. The University of Washington Medical Center, Swedish Medical Center, and Harborview Medical Center are a few of the city's leading medical facilities. These hospitals are outfitted with cutting-edge medical technology and highly qualified medical staff who can offer the required medical care for a variety of ailments and injuries.

Using a telemedicine service is an additional first-aid option for travelers in Seattle. With the convenience of receiving medical treatment from the comfort of their hotel room or home, telemedicine services are growing in popularity. Teladoc, Doctor on Demand, and MDLive are a few notable telemedicine providers in Seattle. With these services, patients have the choice of speaking with a qualified doctor or other healthcare professionals via video chat, phone, or messaging.

Visitors to Seattle have the option of always having a first aid kit on them. In the event of minor injuries or illnesses that don't require immediate medical attention, a first-aid pack might be useful. Band-aids, gauze, antiseptic wipes, pain relievers, and any prescription prescriptions the tourist might need are a few of the crucial supplies that should be contained in a first aid kit.

Therefore, visitors to Seattle should always be ready for emergencies and remember that it's always better to be safe than sorry. Travelers can acquire essential medical care in the event of an emergency by being aware of the emergency contact numbers, visiting urgent care facilities or hospitals, using telemedicine services, and having a first aid kit with them. It's crucial to remember that visitors should always put their safety and well-being first and get medical help when necessary.

Printed in Great Britain
by Amazon

24591611R00090